The French Nobility in Crisis, 1560-1640

The French Nobility in Crisis

1560-1640

DAVIS BITTON

STANFORD UNIVERSITY PRESS
STANFORD, CALIFORNIA
1969

Stanford University Press
Stanford, California
© 1969 by the Board of Trustees of the
Leland Stanford Junior University
Printed in the United States of America
L.C. 69-13177

Preface

In this book I explore contemporary ideas about the French nobility between 1560 and 1640. Although there are studies on other aspects of the French nobility in the sixteenth century, or on the concept of nobility in the eighteenth century, or on ideas about gentility in England or in Italy, there is no work that analyzes what was said in late Renaissance and early modern France regarding the nobility and its role in society. This is regrettable, since the problems of the nobility then evoked a greater amount of controversy than is generally recognized. Although perhaps less exciting than the civil wars, which loom so large in the textbooks, these contemporary debates can tell us a great deal about the values, tensions, and social thought of the period.

Sources for a study of the public image of the nobility in France after 1560 are not scarce. In the *cahiers de doléances*, *plaidoyers*, and *arrêts*, in ballads and satirical poetry, in moralist tracts, in political pamphlets, and in a dozen or so substantial treatises explicitly on the nobility, many detailed problems of class status were argued. I have resisted the temptation to pursue them all, in order to concentrate on the following ones: the nobility's lack of a clearly recognized social function, the difficulty of rationalizing the nobles' legal privileges, the confusion and fluidity of noble status, and the underlying tensions regarding the nature of nobility.

It may be well to state what the book is not. It is not a study of the land market, marriage alliances, the division of family estates, the activities of younger sons, or royal ennoblements. In short, it is not a study of those aspects of the nobility's experience that are essentially external and that, in my view, are best studied on the local level. Their part in the history of the nobility is obvious enough, but those pages that attempt to give an idea of the nobility's economic condition, its military importance, and the like, as a necessary frame of reference, are based on existing studies.

Though contemporary opinions concerning the noble class are not the whole story, their importance should not be hard to recognize. For the question of class relationships and relative social standing can scarcely be understood apart from stereotypes, class self-consciousness, and popular images. Roland Mousnier has reminded us, if we needed reminding, that men often act "less according to the facts themselves than to their mental representation of them."

It is obvious to anyone who has pursued the history of the nobility very far that there was a disconcerting tendency, in different countries and in widely separated centuries, for the same problems to recur. Suspecting that these problems were inherent in the very existence of a privileged hereditary minority attempting to maintain its integrity and its self-esteem, one is constantly lured by the appeals of comparative history. I can only say that although the situation of the French nobility in the late sixteenth and early seventeenth centuries was neither unprecedented nor unparalleled, I have not sought to draw large comparative conclusions.

In order to place the contemporary discussion in its historical context and to compensate for some of the inherent limitations of a topical approach, I have written a preliminary chapter briefly describing the crisis of adjustment the nobility was passing through, explaining the reasons for focusing on the period 1560–1640, and setting the stage for the chapters that follow. Essential to an understanding of the nobility's mood is the whole current of anti-noble sentiment described in Chapter 1.

I have benefited from the advice and encouragement of Professors Joseph R. Strayer, Jerome Blum, and Robert R. Palmer, of Princeton University. Helpful advice on individual chapters was given by Professors John Shy, University of Michigan; J. Russell Major, Emory University; A. Paul Lucas, Washington University at St. Louis; Michel Dassonville, University of Texas; and the late James E. King, University of North Carolina. For counsel and unfaltering patience, I am particularly indebted to the late Professor E. Harris Harbison of Princeton University. The flaws and inadequacies are wholly my own.

In addition to the librarians at Princeton's Firestone Library, I wish to thank those at Yale and at the Columbia University Library's Seligman Collection. Most indispensable of all collections, of course, were those of the Bibliothèque Nationale in Paris, the custodians of which I found to be both efficient and knowledgeable. Finally, I wish to thank my wife and children for their affectionate patience.

D. B.

Contents

The French Nobility in Crisis, 1560-1640

Introduction

Combien les gentilshommes françois sont decheus de ceste ancienne richesse dont leurs maisons estoient ornées sous les regnes de nos bons rois Loys douzième et François Ier!

—François de La Noue (1587)

The French nobles, like the landed aristocracies in other countries, had faced problems of adjustment before. But the period stretching from 1560 to about 1640 was extraordinarily difficult. The transition that the nobility underwent during these years (which was a kind of "identity crisis" with economic and social as well as psychological dimensions) coincided with the basic changes called to mind by such familiar phrases as the age of religious wars, the commercial revolution, and the scientific revolution. It was a crucial phase of the transition from the French nobility of the late Middle Ages to the French nobility of the Old Regime. To be sure, the noble class had often shown symptoms of insecurity and maladjustment earlier in its history, but it was during the *crise de classe* of the late sixteenth and early seventeenth centuries that its problems became most acute—converging, and causing the inherent dilemmas of privileged aristocracy to stand out in bold relief. Above all, it was during these years, to judge from the *cahiers,* pamphlets, and treatises then published, that Frenchmen were more self-conscious, aware, and articulate regarding the nobility's problems than they had ever been before.

The nobility was suffering economically. There had been a decline in seigneurial income ever since the end of the Hun-

dred Years' War; but not until the great price revolution of
the sixteenth century, the effects of which began to be felt in
France in the 1520's, did most nobles experience an alarming
decline in real income. Soon incomes of only 1,000 or even 500
livres a year were not at all uncommon.[1] The inevitable result
was heavy indebtedness. The French nobility was "criblée de
dettes," said the Venetian ambassador in 1569.[2] Another observer estimated that eight out of ten noble families had either
lost property or gone seriously into debt. Differ as they might
on other questions, contemporaries usually agreed that the
nobility's economic situation was far from comfortable.[3]

To be sure, some historians have challenged the traditional
view of the nobility's decline.[4] But there is enough evidence
of indebtedness, of the sale of estates, of the disappearance of
family names from the ranks of the nobility to prohibit us
from maintaining that the order as a whole was fundamentally prosperous. And there is enough evidence of actual suffering to prevent us from writing off as deliberate prevarica-
tion the vociferous complaints of the old nobility. For whatever reasons, a sense of economic constriction was present.

Almost as painful as the economic decline, and closely connected with it, were the increasing incursions of non-nobles
into the ranks of the nobility. There had always been the possibility of crossing class lines, of course, but the possibility was
realized more and more often in the early sixteenth century.
Since such active social mobility (which we shall examine in
Chapter 6) was a direct consequence of economic changes, it is
not surprising that it reached a point of extraordinary inten-
sity in the 1550's.

Suffering from economic decline and from social incursions,
the nobility of France was also experiencing a galling form of
"unemployment." It had been traditional for noblemen,
younger sons especially, to spend time in the military service.
Not only had this practice relieved some of the pressure on
the family estates but it had given the nobility a vague but
reassuring sense of usefulness, of class pride. Unfortunately,

however, changes in the nature of warfare were lessening the importance of mounted warriors, and the transformation of armies (considered in Chapter 2) was accelerated during the sixteenth century.

So, by the 1550's, just before this study begins, the nobility was experiencing severe discomfort. Then came new convulsions. Starting in 1557 an acute economic crisis brought considerable social dislocation. In 1559, when the peace treaty of Cateau-Cambrésis ended the Hapsburg-Valois wars, hundreds of noble sons were thrown back on the home estates, where the family resources were often insufficient to support them. Bands of armed noblemen roamed the countryside, pillaging and plundering.[5] Small wonder that some nobles, looking back through the years nostalgically, later saw the reigns of Francis I and Henry II as idyllic.[6] The troubles of the nobility were not strictly new, but around the middle of the century they seemed more acute than ever before.

The decades following 1560 were turbulent and confused. It was the age of religious wars, of factional quarrels and civil strife. There were kidnappings, drownings, massacres, and assassinations. In a way, the very turmoil of the age adds to its interest for the history of the nobility. Precisely because it was not a period of stability and calm, the possibility of working out new patterns, social as well as political and religious, seemed less remote than usual. More important, it was an age of unusual articulateness. Religious differences were argued heatedly and endlessly. Political and constitutional questions inspired a prodigious outpouring of words. Attempts were being made to bring about reform of the customary law, a program bound to raise many social questions. Between 1560 and 1614 the Estates General were called together for several clamorous sessions. Books, pamphlets, tracts, and broadsides appeared in great numbers. It seemed that everyone was taking pen in hand, as one modern historian has said, "to reform or reconstruct society."[7]

It would be remarkable indeed, in such an atmosphere, if

nothing were said about the nobility. As a matter of fact, a great deal was said about the nobility and its role. Tiraqueau's great treatise on nobility, first published in 1549, aroused sufficient interest that new editions were brought out in 1559, 1566, 1572, 1573, 1584, 1597, 1602, and 1617. Other large treatises, notably those of L'Alouëte in 1577, Du Rivault in 1596, Thierriat in 1606, and Loyseau in 1608, 1610, and 1613, analyzed noble status and its meaning. Many pamphlets and small ephemeral works also expressed views on the nobility's situation. In Dauphiny, as we shall see in Chapter 1, a vigorous public controversy regarding the nobility and its privileges kept tempers warm for several decades. The cahiers prepared for the Estates General (like those for some of the provincial Estates) almost always contained substantial sections on "la noblesse." Legal commentaries, collections of litigation, and royal ordinances all had much to say on the meaning of noble status. By the beginning of the seventeenth century a prominent jurist could observe that no other subject of French law had been so worked over as that of noble status.[8]

Many of the issues that had been discussed earlier were raised anew in the context of the Estates General of 1614 and during the years before Louis XIII asserted his rule. I have tried to discover how this debate regarding the nobility's role worked itself out during the 1620's and 1630's, but I have not plunged forward into the 1640's and the complicated struggles of the Fronde. This study, then, considers the seventy or eighty years extending from about 1560 through the 1630's.

The French nobility was complex and sprawling. Unlike the peerage in England, it was not limited to a few holders of titles; younger sons in France were not placed apart in some kind of "gentry" but were considered full-fledged nobles. Moreover, there were new nobles of various kinds and even quasi-nobles, i.e., people who were considered to have almost noble status. Most of these distinctions will be ignored throughout the following chapters. We are dealing with contemporary social thought, and more often than not contemporaries spoke simply of "the nobility." In most instances, as one can tell by the context, they meant the "old" nobility or the "nobility of the sword." Or they meant simply the Second Estate as a whole. The newer subgroups, after all, usually wished to melt into the existing aristocracy and not to stand out as an unnatural appendage. It is important, of course, to be aware of the complexity and fluidity of social status under the Old Regime, and "the ambiguity of noble status" will be explored in a later chapter. In general, however, we can best appreciate how contemporaries saw the role of the nobility by following their own, usually undifferentiated terminology.

All things considered, the dialogue on the nobility and its role was both lively and varied. Contemporaries discussed every conceivable question, from how class status was transmitted at the time of Noah to what credentials were required to gain exemption from tax levies. Some of these questions, the ones that seem the most basic, will be taken up in the following chapters.

CHAPTER I

Anti-Noble Sentiment

Que les gentilzhommes oyseuz et sans service au Roy
payent tailles comme les roturiers.
—A demand from Epernay (1560)

Le laboreur foulé deteste la noblesse.
—ANTOINE DU VERDIER (1572)

Ils prennent la noblesse pour une mauvaise herbe en
vostre Royaume, et la veulent empescher de multiplier.
—PIERRE DE BOYSSAT (1603)

Before turning to the contemporary discussion of the nobility's role specifically, it will be helpful to become familiar
with the anti-noble sentiment of the late sixteenth and early
seventeenth centuries. Not new in the strict sense, such hostility now became persistent and unprecedentedly strident—
ranging from denouncing noble excesses and sniping at the
traditional exemptions to making lofty generalizations about
equality in the abstract. Without knowing this background,
it would be difficult indeed to understand the nobility's hyper-
sensitivity, its defensive mentality, its awkward efforts to provide a convincing rationalization of its privileges.

I

The fact that there was hostility toward the nobles is evident enough from several outbreaks of violence. In 1579, there
was a revolt against the nobles of Dauphiny. In 1590, some
nobles of Brittany were massacred, and the enraged peasants
wanted to kill all other nobles as well.[1] In 1595, the revolt of
the "Croquants" broke out in Perigord, where another rising
followed in 1599. Several similar events occurred in Guienne.

Although the revolts were seldom, if ever, motivated purely and simply by popular hatred of the nobility, this factor bulked sufficiently large to arouse apprehension in the hearts of the nobles, some of whom had visions of being forced into servitude, overthrown, or exterminated.[2] They dared not allow the peasants to bear arms for fear of the "consequences" and "inconveniences" that might result.[3]

But this does not take us very far. The risings must be seen as part of a tradition going back to the fourteenth century or before. In themselves they tell us more about the temperature of the hostility than its nature. If we would understand the popular resentment of the nobility in the late sixteenth and early seventeenth century, we must see it, first of all, against a background of "feudal intensification," a vigorous effort by the seigneurs to increase their manorial revenue. From one point of view, this effort—which in practice meant increasing the demands on the peasants—may be regarded as merely one of the several ways in which the landed aristocracy attempted to adjust to the long secular price rise of the sixteenth century and to counteract the decline of its real income. Even if it were conducted with tact and restraint, however, the effort could not fail to provoke resentment. And since all too often it degenerated into oppression and abuse, it is not surprising that the nobles were vigorously criticized.*

In 1560, the general cahier of the Third Estate contained a scathing denunciation of nobles who were arbitrarily subjecting their peasants to greater demands, not only by requiring payment of old obligations ignored in the past, but also by illicitly imposing many new ones. The peasants, it said, were forced to work on special *corvées,* for which they received no payment, and to turn over quantities of farm produce "under color of some special pretended right to which they [the nobles] have no title except usurpation."[4]

---

* All landowners were not nobles, to be sure, but many of them were, and the others pretended to be; criticism was almost always directed against "the nobles."

Ordinances were issued against such practices, but since they were seldom enforced, they merely provide additional evidence of what the grievances were. In 1579, all nobles who did not have the legal right of corvée were forbidden to force their peasants to perform "charroiz, labours, façons de vigne, faulchemens de prez et aultres oeuvres quelzconques" (cart-service, vineyard work, and the like), and were required to limit their demands to voluntary service for which the peasants would be reasonably paid. Nobles who did have the rights of corvée were forbidden to compel additional service, to impose new dues, to deprive peasants of their traditional pasture and common land, or to intimidate *métayers* who were working for others.[5] At about the same time, the Estates of Brittany denounced certain nobles for imposing unjust exactions, and in 1589, the Third Estate of Berry demanded that seigneurs guilty of requiring new corvées be deprived of their fiefs.[6]

It was not only the imposition of unjust dues that aroused resentment. Even more irritating were the blatant ruses used to maintain the appearance of legality. The general cahier of the Third Estate described some of these methods: a nobleman might exact exorbitant material and labor contributions under the pretext of saving his peasants from marauding troops; he might have an accomplice pick a quarrel with an unfortunate peasant, whereupon the nobleman could invade (and plunder) the property under the pretext of "keeping the peace"; or he might lodge soldiers in the homes of uncooperative peasants under the pretext of wartime necessity.[7] Oppression and maltreatment of peasants, said François de La Noue, seemed to be regarded by some as one of the marks of nobility.[8]

In 1614, an anonymous pamphleteer wrote that the nobility was almost always oppressive and sometimes unbearable, that the peasants were beaten not only for failing to perform cart-service but even for failing to show proper deference, and that by threats or force a peasant could be made to sell his land or to marry his daughter to one of the nobleman's servants. "If war returns," nobles were reported to have muttered, "we will teach these gray feet to respect the nobility."[9] One can sense not only the nobility's concern for its declining prestige but also the indignation that the misbehavior of nobles had aroused.

But harshness toward one's own peasants was only part of the excesses charged to the nobility. In 1560, François Grimaudet, a lawyer of the king at Angers, spoke of nobles who went into the villages to beat and steal and "to do much violence against the people."[10] And in 1573, the diocese of Castres complained of nobles who allowed crimes to go unpunished, protected guilty parties, and themselves committed numerous acts of oppression.[11] Particularly impressive is the evidence supplied by the special courts known as the Grands-Jours. The royal statement calling a session of the Grands-Jours at Poitiers, in 1579, states that the court was summoned because of the backlog of litigation and because of the excesses committed by "the nobles and others of our subjects."[12] This special mention of nobles seems justified in view of the subsequent findings of the court. For nobles were found guilty—not in rare instances but repeatedly—of murder, extortion, assault, looting, seizing ecclesiastical property, intimidating and manhandling royal agents who tried to enforce order, and taking refuge, when indicted, behind the castle walls of their fellow noblemen.[13] Nor were the crimes and enormities confined to Poitou. Nicolas de Crest claimed that there were at least 500 nobles in Bordelais who had each been responsible for the death of over one hundred persons; that some 250 nobles in Touraine had turned the unsettled conditions to their profit and had been protected in their excesses by corrupt officials; and that throughout the country, if six chambers of the Grands-Jours worked at full speed, it would take three years to catch up on the complaints dealing with major crimes alone.[14] Although the figures may be inflated, the general impression of widespread misbehavior by nobles remains.

It could be argued, of course, that the crimes and excesses were due not to any special perversity of the nobles, but rather to the license and anarchy of the civil wars. In a letter describing the Grands-Jours of Clermont, the eminent jurist-antiquarian Estienne Pasquier mentioned that he was not surprised at the "deportment of the nobility" when he considered "the nature of the place where it is situated [Auvergne], a mountainous country as far removed from the light of the king as from the court of Parlement, plus the ravages that our civil wars have brought for over twenty-two years, during which the nobles have always had weapons in hand, and no military discipline."[15] Pasquier did not think that courts of law could do much good in the midst of hostilities, and he cautioned against being too hard on the nobles by digging up old crimes or by giving credence to rumor and calumny.

A similar attempt to explain the nobility's behavior in terms of the wartime conditions was that of Bernard Du Haillan, a royal servant best known for his account of late-sixteenth-century France. In 1570, he described the nobility as "honored and revered by the people" and "in such fear of the law that it would not think of mistreating its subjects."[16] A few years later, in the revised edition of his work, he inserted the following explanation: "That was before, but since then our nobility has become exceedingly licentious. It is the time that brought this license; another time will take it away and will cause the nobility to return to what it was."[17]

But such reasoning did little to diminish popular condemnation of the nobility. For one thing, peace did not always bring surcease. The nobles were scarcely models of respect for the law, even, as the diocese of Castres had complained, "in time of peace." And as late as 1614 a petition to the Estates General complained that while the rest of the kingdom enjoyed complete peace, the peasants were beaten, imprisoned, and killed. "A great many acts of inhumanity are being committed," they continued, "and no one has taken our cause in hand."[18]

Besides, the wartime conditions were scarcely a believable excuse for the nobility's misdeeds when it was often precisely the nobles who were blamed for the civil wars. In 1562, soon after the outbreak of fighting, Claude Haton said that the Huguenots who rebelled against the king were "for the most part noblemen"; if *roturiers* (non-nobles) were guilty of some of the same crimes, this was due to "following the example of the nobles or serving them."[19] But it was not only Huguenot nobles who were blamed for the troubles. In 1573, according to a complaint from the diocese of Narbonne, "Most of the nobility, even though they proudly claim to be Catholics in the service of the king, wage war disgracefully.... It appears that the nobles and the enemy have sworn to bring about the total ruin of the people."[20] At times those who blamed the nobles for the wars even spoke darkly of some kind of aristocratic conspiracy. It was reported from Dauphiny that "the pillaging soldiers very rarely attacked noble property even though the owner was of the enemy camp."[21] Similar conditions were reported from Languedoc by Fourquevaux:

The common opinion is . . . that the civil wars would have been already extinguished in Languedoc if the nobility that calls itself Catholic had wanted to put forth any effort to resist the rebels.... In the party of the rebels there are noblemen who have relatives, allies, and friends among our Catholic nobles.... They openly help each other; the one group holds the lamb while the other cuts its throat.[22]

A complaint from Montpellier was even more pointed: "It is easy to see that the further continuation of the civil wars is caused by the support, dissimulation, and connivance of the nobility."[23]

Since crimes were also committed by non-nobles, to condemn only the nobility may seem unfair. Certainly the bands of pillagers during the civil wars often included roturiers. Our concern here, however, is not to apportion responsibility, but to learn something of how the nobles were regarded by contemporaries. And without any question there was a tendency to blame them for the wars in general and for the violence committed by armed bands. Even when not specifically charged with the rapine, somehow they were considered responsible. As the royal advisor and jurist François de L'Alouëte, said:

The nobles have really perverted the use of the sword. For even though it does not belong to them, and it is not for themselves that they carry it, they use it every day for nothing but avenging their own passions and quarrels. And they hold the law and those who administer it in such disdain that they speak of them only with contempt. . . . Evil men break the rules and pervert the law and no one stops them. Violence and oppression are rampant throughout France, while the nobleman laughs and rests at his ease.[24]

Here the nobles were being condemned for allowing as well as for committing crimes. It could be argued that all nobles were not guilty and that generalization was therefore unjustified. The nobles of Dauphiny, for example, conceded that the Third Estate had reason to complain of certain individual nobles but not of all.

And yet they [the Third Estate] would cast the blame on all . . . and would consume both the malefactor and the innocent, making no distinction between their benefactors and their enemies. . . . Even though those who are guilty be nobles, it is not valid to impute [the crimes] to the entire nobility. The act of the individual cannot be extended to apply to the general.[25]

We can sympathize with the nobles who made this complaint; the generalization was indeed being made. The satirical verse of the period provides some good examples. In 1562, Ronsard wondered whether the nobility, who anciently received their titles from the king, were now going to destroy the kingdom.[26] In 1565, Jacques Bereau, after repeating the commonplace that the nobles had long defended France, asked if they were now going to turn upon her.[27] In 1572, the popular reaction to pillage was described by Antoine Du Verdier:

> Le laboreur foulé deteste la noblesse:
> Au lieu d'allegement, dict-il, elle nous blesse.
> J'ay eu, en trois logis, de soldats trente neuf
> Qui ne m'ont delaissé veau, brebis, poule n'oeuf.[28]

In 1585, Guillaume de Buys, after describing the nobility at some length, expressed a common reaction to the outrages:

> Le Cynique, aussi bien, à qui tout est permis
> Ceste umbre de noblesse en tel rang il a mis
> Qu'il dit que ce n'est rien que belle couverture
> De meurdre, de pillage, et de tort, et d'injure.[29]

Balthazar Bailly, another poet who deplored the brutality of the age, likewise assigned the responsibility to the nobility.[30]

There may be some poetic license here, to be sure, but equally sharp criticism can be found in the most sober and legalistic prose. For example, a statement from the bailliage of Epernay: "The nobility is today so unrestrained and devoid of reason that its justice consists in sword thrusts and murders."[31] Even the Grands-Jours of 1579, which as a judicial body was concerned with individual infractions, summed up its findings with a general statement: "The nobility is extremely dissolute."[32]

Perhaps the significance of these general denunciations can best be appreciated by recalling an observation of the late Professor Johan Huizinga. Referring to conditions in the fourteenth and fifteenth centuries, he remarked that "to the catholic soul the unworthiness of the persons never compromises the sacred character of the institution." Thus "the spectacle of a violent and dissipated nobility" did not hinder "the veneration of the order in itself."[33] Yet the number of those who denounced not only individuals but also "la noblesse" increased. More and more people did not "venerate" the order, to say the least, and were coming to have strong doubts about its "sacred character." This becomes particularly obvious when we turn from the denunciation of oppression and bellicosity to complaints about the nobility's traditional tax exemptions.

II

Over and over again the cahiers of the late sixteenth century demanded that the king "maintain the nobility in its traditional privileges and exemptions." Since this demand was normally conceded by clergy, Third Estate, and king alike, one might assume that the nobility had no cause for anxiety and that its defense of its exemptions was merely formal. But to the nobles themselves their privileges seemed far from secure. Not even the most basic and cherished of these, exemption from paying the *taille,* was going unchallenged.*

There were, of course, sound reasons for calling the noble privileges into question. A long-term shifting of the traditional functions of the noble class had undermined the rationale upon which its exemptions were based. Many nonnobles, however, saw the exemptions simply as a financial disadvantage, increasing the burden on themselves and decreasing the revenue of the crown. There seems to have come, in the late sixteenth century, a heightened awareness that the burden on the taxpayers varied in direct proportion to the number of exemptions. The legist Cardin LeBret, in one of his *plaidoyers,* remarked that the proposed ennoblement of a roturier holding in Brittany would penalize the rest of the parish.[34] On another occasion, he urged the king to be re-

---

* The taille was the most important direct tax in France and almost always the single largest source of revenue for the crown. Through a complicated process of apportionment, specific assessments were made on provinces, generalities, parishes, and finally individuals. In theory one paid according to his wealth, including both real estate and income, but there were many inequities, both geographical and individual. The large numbers of exemptions—which were applied to the nobility, the clergy, many towns, and many of the most affluent bourgeois—combined with inefficient and sometimes corrupt collection practices to make the taille a source of irritation throughout the Old Regime.

strained in granting exemptions because they would throw an undue charge on those who still had to pay. He found it "shocking" that there were almost as many exempt as tax-payers:

It should at least be considered that when they were granted this exemption the tailles were so moderate that it was very easy for even the most needy to pay them without having cause for complaint. But since they have now been increased to thirty times what they were at the beginning, would it not be reasonable either to diminish the number of privileged (instead of increasing them as is done every day) or at least during time of national necessity to have them bear a certain part of the charge in order to relieve the peasants?[35]

To be sure, most often it was the non-noble *privilégiés* who were under attack. Local decisions that the non-noble clergy should be subjected to the taille, complaints that the nobles were obtaining exemptions for their tenants, servants, and hired help, complaints against the swarm of officeholders, widespread disapproval of the increasing number of *anoblis* (persons ennobled by the king), frequent demands that "false nobles" of different kinds be subjected to the taille—all this may have struck too close for comfort, but it would be wrong to see it as a frontal attack on the privileged position of the old nobility.

Nevertheless more radical ideas were in the air. In 1560, the Third Estate of Epernay had demanded that "gentlemen who are idle and of no service to the king pay tailles as roturiers do." Three years later the demand from Epernay was yet more sweeping: let the "taille be levied on all of the inhabitants, clerical, noble, and lay."[36] In 1567, a nobleman noted with horror a proposal to impose a uniform income tax of five percent on everyone, nobles and non-nobles alike. "They will make us all villeins," he said, "or at least will treat us as villeins."[37]

The threat to exemptions came from above as well as from

below, for the kings and those concerned with the government's financial needs also came to take an increasingly dim view of excessive exemptions. This is not surprising. The resources of the crown, which had never been abundant, were extraordinarily straitened in the late sixteenth century; and the system of taxation, notoriously confused and badly administered, was simply not meeting the needs of wartime and emergency expenses. Appropriately, many of the proposals for increasing revenue were concerned with methods of collection. In addition there were significant efforts, especially in the Estates General of 1588 and the Assemblies of Notables of 1597 and 1617, to increase the number of *taillables*.[38] The exemptions of the anoblis and the officeholders were curtailed, as by the edict of January 1598; earlier, Henry III even went so far as to advocate sweeping aside the old system and imposing in its place a general hearth tax on all the households of the kingdom.[39] This was not done, but the implications of such a scheme were revolutionary indeed; the nobles had good reason to squirm.

As a matter of fact, the nobles were actually paying taxes, the emergency imposts of wartime. In theory this did not impair their exemption from the regular taxes under normal conditions, but often this was small comfort. In 1567, a nobleman complained that the terms used to describe these irregular levies, such as subventions and aids, were more pleasing to the ear than the word "tailles," but that the effects were "no less cruel and rigorous."[40] In 1560, when the nobles demanded that they be exempted from "all taxes, old and new, of whatever kind they might be," the king replied that as soon as possible he would abolish the ones they had to pay "because of the necessities of war."[41]

In Brittany, an interesting case in point, the question of whether the nobility's traditional tax exemptions would apply to the new taxes troubled the province for several years. A series of abnormally heavy demands by the king had aroused an interest there in extending the tax base to include the nobility. In 1572, the question of the nobility's contribution arose when the king requested 960,000 livres, to be raised over a period of six years. The nobles sought to have their exemptions recognized in the provincial Estates; but the Third Estate would not allow it, and the question remained unresolved for the next two years. Then, with the province still trying to raise the money, the king decreed that non-nobles must pay while those who were "truly nobles" need not pay.[42] Although this decree would seem to have decided the question, a forced loan was imposed on everyone four years later—"neither the churchmen nor the nobles were exempted."[43] In 1579, despite the nobility's appeals to the king, the Brittany Estates decided that all should pay the tax of that year, "of whatever quality or condition they might be."[44]

Finally, not the least of the threats to the nobility's exemptions were demands that the taxes and exemptions be attached to land rather than to persons. This arrangement, known as *taille réelle*, already existed in Languedoc, Provence, and a few other localities of the south and west. It provided that roturiers need pay no tax on the "noble" lands they held, whereas nobles were liable to taxation for their "roturier" lands. It was subject to abuse, but on the whole taille réelle had the advantage of predictability, and it avoided some of the more obvious inconveniences of the prevailing system of *taille personelle*.[45]

Most of the agitation for extending taille réelle was in the central and southern provinces. The village of Blaigny, for instance, demanded in 1576 that the tax be paid not only by all roturiers but also by those nobles who held lands "en roture."[46] Similar demands were heard in Guienne, in Normandy, and, most loudly, in Dauphiny. On one occasion at least it was proposed that taille réelle be extended to all of the kingdom.[47] The issues were complex, but certainly the reform, had it been implemented, would have relieved the Third Estate of part of its tax burdens, and would have weakened the personal exemptions of the nobility.

In short, the nobility's anxiety over its exemptions was not without cause. For in addition to the general jostling, there were successful efforts to tax the nobles for wartime expenses, less successful efforts to tax them for their roturier lands, and a few broad demands that they pay the taille as everyone else did. Taken all together, the pressure was at least disquieting.

III

Many of the facets of anti-noble sentiment, including the attacks on exemptions, can be seen most clearly in Dauphiny, where a controversy over the question of taille réelle extended over a period of many years. Here as nowhere else there was a sharp clash of class interests, and the latent hostility toward the nobility came out into the open.

The issue of taille réelle had been raised in Dauphiny as early as the 1530's and then again in the 1550's. On those occasions the Third Estate had not been united, and nothing had been achieved. When the controversy broke out again in the 1590's, however, the alignment was simple—the Third Estate vs. the privileged orders. Both sides prepared carefully reasoned briefs. Spokesmen presented their cases before Henry IV in 1595, and later before the royal council; at the same time they made a more general appeal for support through a remarkable series of pamphlets. Here the clash between nobles and non-nobles was direct and articulate.

To gain a sense of this unique confrontation in Dauphiny, let us consider the major areas of dispute and the arguments used by both sides.

1. *The historical argument*, or argument from precedent. The nobility regarded its privileges as having been firmly established in centuries past, and argued that these had been reaffirmed by the agreement that made Dauphiny part of France, by a later convention of 1554, and by a decision of Catherine de Médicis in 1579. The Third Estate, on the other hand, regarded the privileges as belonging to the province, not only to the privileged orders; it dismissed the convention of

1554 as being due to coercion, and described the queen mother's decision as due to special interests and therefore invalid. In an effort to establish the antiquity of taille réelle in Dauphiny, the Third Estate presented an abstruse interpretation of the meaning of the ancient listings of hearths. Both sides argued with immense patience and concern for historical detail.

More important to us, however, than the bare arguments are the overtones of resentment. To explain how the nobles had managed to have the tailles of recent years collected on a "personal" basis, it was said that often no one dared to defy the nobles in the villages and that the Estates General had been under the domination of the first two orders, who thus had been able to slip in the clause making nobles personally exempt.[48]

The Third Estate's argument from history was perhaps its weakest position; and it is in some of the other arguments that the attitudes toward the nobility show most clearly.

2. *Changing conditions.* The Third Estate confessed its lack of confidence in the historical argument in a way by insisting that custom and precedent were not decisive. "Those who would make a shield of custom against reason," it said, "fail to consider that by so doing they are establishing the greatest and most cruel tyranny in the world."[49] The nobility, on the other hand, thought in terms of a contract that could not be broken unilaterally, changing conditions or not.

3. *The nobility's military obligation.* If the nobles wished to adhere strictly to the conditions of their privileged status, said the Third Estate, let them remember that those conditions were established in return for their military service. They now fell far short of the performance that once had justified their preferential treatment. Under present conditions, therefore, the nobility should not enjoy exemption as a class. This argument, which the nobility of Dauphiny seems to have ignored, will make more sense in the context of the next chapter.

4. *The common-burden argument.* It should be noted that

the arguments thus far considered could be used not only to make nobles pay taxes for their roturier lands (which was the meaning of taille réelle) but for their noble lands as well. This is also true of the common-burden argument, which held that since the catastrophe of war had fallen upon all alike it was unfair for the expenses to be borne by the Third Estate alone. If three people were in a storm-tossed ship, should one of them save the other two? Should not all of them contribute equally to their common effort to be saved? The traditional maritime law should be applied in such cases: any property jettisoned in order to save the ship must be paid for by all the passengers.[50]

This argument was meant to apply, I believe, only to war expenses. But the Third Estate was not always perfectly clear about this, sometimes demanding that the nobles help pay for the expenses of wartime and for "affaires communes." Recognizing that such an argument, carried to its logical conclusions, would destroy their exemptions entirely, the nobility reiterated the tired claim that their share was provided by military service.

5. *The inequities of taille personelle.* Here we come to what was certainly the basic reason for the Third Estate's crusade, or at least for its recurrence in the 1590's, and, interestingly enough, the only argument bearing directly on taille réelle as opposed to taille personelle. Evidently the losses of war had forced many roturiers to sell their lands for practically nothing to nobles. This was, I judge, a fairly recent development, since throughout the sixteenth century the general direction of land sales, in Dauphiny as elsewhere, was from noble to roturier. At any rate, the sales created an intolerable situation for those roturiers who did not sell; the taille being personal (i.e. only on roturiers), the number of taxpayers was decreasing while the amount levied remained constant. Thus one person who did not even possess a single hearth was forced to pay for ten others who had sold their property to nobles and moved away.[51]

The Third Estate's solution was for the king to declare Dauphiny a province of taille réelle, thus giving it only the same consideration already enjoyed by Languedoc and Provence. Nobles would then pay the taille on any roturier lands they held, which they should not object to since they were willing enough to put roturiers on the *ban et arrière-ban* rolls for any noble lands they might hold.[52] The transfer of property across class lines would then neither increase nor decrease the tax base. Everyone should be content.

But the nobility was far from content with the proposal. They claimed their old rights, appealed to custom, and insisted that whatever injustices had been done should not be blamed on the nobility as a class. Let us differentiate, they said, between those few nobles who have taken advantage of conditions by obtaining roturier lands for next to nothing and the many other nobles who have acquired nothing, or only a little and at a reasonable price. The regular channels of justice were available for redress of specific grievances—"without punishing the entire order of the nobility."[53] If nobles had been guilty of exploiting roturier misfortunes, so also had merchants, lawyers, and officeholders. Therefore, they said, let us try more moderate measures that will not make a scapegoat of the nobility. Finally, they added that the Third Estate was not consistent: for years roturiers had been buying up noble lands (and paying a roturier's taxes) without protest, yet now that things had changed in the past five or six years, they raised a wail of complaint. As for Languedoc and Provence, their customs were different; it would be better to look at examples among the provinces of the center, north, and west.

In addition to these major arguments, the nobles' excesses during the wars provided grounds for complaint. Again, for the Third Estate, the solution was to get rid of the nobility's "usurped exemption."[54]

The Dauphiny conflict reveals some basic attitudes. Clearly, the Third Estate's antagonism toward the nobility was often intense. There was little inclination to be respectful or obsequious toward the nobles, who were vigorously denounced for everything from distorting the laws by coercion and pressure to mistreating the common people and failing to assume their fair share of the state's burden. As the debate became more heated, the spokesmen of the Third Estate (mainly writers of pamphlets and delegates to provincial estates) uttered poorly disguised threats: "The nobility would be well advised not to provoke the anger and vengeance of God upon them, for sooner or later He will avenge this oppression."[55] Many members of the Third Estate emphatically felt, and sometimes said, that they were as good as the nobles. Consider the obvious sarcasm of the following: the nobles would pay the taille only for their roturier lands; of course if they held no such lands they would not find themselves "soiled or infected, as they fear, from touching or mingling" with roturiers.[56] It is evident that roturiers were sometimes irritated by the nobility's assumptions of superiority.

Despite its disavowal of wishing to do away with the nobility, the Third Estate made many arguments that went far beyond the mere demand for taille réelle. Although at times it was clear on what must be considered its serious position—that nobles could remain exempt for their noble lands except in time of war—at other times it was not at all so clear. With respect to each of the major types of impositions, for example, the Third Estate once described the liability of the different orders as follows. (1) "Dons" (extraordinary aids)—to be paid by all orders alike. (2) Impositions for common defense—to be paid by all orders alike. (3) Tailles—all subjects of Dauphiny to be exempt from the so-called extraordinary tailles, while all should pay the ordinary tailles. It is difficult to find in this schema just what special exemptions the nobility would enjoy. It must have been small comfort to discover elsewhere in the Third Estate's argument that the nobility's liability to ordinary tailles would have been only for roturier lands and only in the eventuality that taille réelle was recognized in Dauphiny. On one occasion at least, in 1576, there had been talk of imposing the taille on all classes alike, without qualification.[57]

Moreover, the arguments from history, changing conditions, the nobility's feeble military performance, and the common burden, if allowed, obviously could have resulted in the loss of all special noble exemptions. The agitation for taille réelle, in this context and buttressed by such arguments, was, whether intended or not, a frontal attack on that which was most valued by the nobility.

Finally, it is worth noting that in the eyes of some nobles the attacks were inspired by ideas of social equality, by a desire to destroy the nobility. The "obstinate efforts" against them, they explained, were due to "an envy long burning under the warm coals of hate and malevolence."[58] They feared that their sacrifices during the wars would be repaid by "the destruction of the first two orders in order to save the Third."[59] They noted that some rich roturiers had entered the noble class "by breaking the barriers of their condition," while others, equally wealthy, remained outside the noble ranks and sought comfort in "the maxim that nature created us all equal."[60]

Discussions of the idea of equality or the "destruction" of the nobility were infrequent and should decidedly not be regarded as "typical" of popular sentiment. For one thing, we have been dealing exclusively with negative attitudes toward the nobility. These may have been a minority report. It would be idle to pretend that everyone was obsessed with hatred of the nobles. A large proportion of the population, either indifferent or preoccupied with other concerns, probably did not feel strongly about the nobility one way or the other. And undoubtedly the peasants on some estates were well treated, and the relations between them and the seigneur harmonious.[61]

Even the criticism of the nobility and the expressions of hostility that we have considered were usually not equalitarian in their emphasis. The denunciation of the nobles' oppression and pillage almost never included any demands for social equality; a less unruly nobility still in full possession of its privileges would apparently have satisfied most critics. Even the pressures to bring the nobles under some form of taxation, as potentially revolutionary as they were, were almost never accompanied by demands for full equality. Still, the idea of equality was in the air. Although not usually defined, the word was used. It was common, for example, for rich roturiers to cite Seneca's statement that all men are created equal.[62] The passage was frequently repeated, as we can gather from the demurrers' tone of impatience: "I cannot share the opinion of those who have said that Nature created all men equal," said Le Bret, "even though they base their opinion on the authority of Seneca."[63] And Mayerne, whose views on the social structure were basically bourgeois, insisted that inequality was natural, for "the Creator of all things did not make his works all equal."[64] Often Plato (who had compared human differences to the differences among clay, iron, and silver) was called in to offset the authority of Seneca.

The subject was not entirely a harmless topic for parlor conversation among classicists. Behind the high-flown abstractions were harsh realities. The impoverishment of many nobles, the uprisings, the criticism, the attempts to tax nobles—all had to be regarded with some seriousness. The nobles were seldom in a mood to be amused by talk of equality. In a speech before the noble delegates at the Estates General of 1614, one of the spokesmen for the Third Estate compared the three orders of the kingdom to three brothers, adding that sometimes the youngest son turns out to be the savior of his older brothers. Outraged at this comparison, the nobles stormed and fumed, complained to the king, and demanded a formal apology. After a series of conferences, deputations, and patient explanations, aided by the mediation of the king, the queen mother, and the clergy, the delegates were finally able to get down to the more important business of preparing their respective general cahiers.[65]

On the surface it seems absurd that time and energy were

lost over such a question. But although the delegates of the Third Estate explicitly stated and restated their respect for the nobility, they also insisted that the Third Estate was no less important to the country than the nobles, and they did use a metaphor that implied a kind of equality among the three orders. Less than a decade later, a curious anonymous work contained the following words: "I say of the bourgeois that he is only slightly lower than the nobility—and if I were to say equal, I don't know that I would be wrong."[66] Such statements touched a tender nerve.

Some people thought they saw a giant conspiracy to overthrow the nobility. They spoke of the French nobles receiving "the Swiss treatment."[67] They noticed the general lack of affection, and concluded that if the people tried "to raise its horns," it would have to be resisted.[68]

Not surprisingly, the equalitarian ferment was blamed on the Protestants. The nobles of Gascony denounced the Protestants for wishing to bring the other estates—and "principally the nobility"—into servitude.[69] In 1574, the hearts of many nobles must have been chilled by a prediction of what would happen in the event of a Protestant victory:

In order for us to see what would happen if we were reduced to that extremity, I have only to tell of a synod that was held at Challons-sur-la-Saone at the beginning of the troubles, where a large number of ministers concluded that their religion could not be firmly established without first exterminating three types of vermin: the church of the papists, the Parlements, and the nobility. And as a matter of fact, according to the instructions and ordinances of the ministers, several houses of noblemen were burned by their own peasants.[70]

We see how nobles are treated at Geneva, the pamphlet continued. If the Catholic Church is replaced by such a religion, where would that leave us? On what could we base our nobility? If we cited the ordinances of kings and emperors, the ministers would reply that "they are human inventions, that by the law of grace and according to the purity of the gospel all men are born free, and that nothing should be admitted that is not contained explicitly in the scriptures, where we do not find this word gentleman."[71] In 1590, Cardinal Cajetan published a pamphlet of open letters "to the nobility of France." The Protestants, he said, wanted nothing more than to "oppress the nobility and to ride roughshod over it more than any other estate." As for the Catholics, he explained: "I assure you that the slightest thought of preferring the people to the nobility has never entered our minds."[72]

These partisan statements are not accurate descriptions of the churches' attitudes toward social classes. On the whole, Protestant thought was more conservative—and more complex—than the above charges would indicate. But it is obvious that the specter of social equality was arousing apprehension. Even if aristocratic fears of leveling radicalism were out of proportion to the threat, nonetheless nobles were being attacked and criticized on various levels and more and more frequently. It is against this background that their uneasiness, touchiness, and anxiety, their desire to regain a recognized social function, and their efforts to explain and justify their privileged position begin to become intelligible.

CHAPTER 2

Military Service

La forme propre, et seule, et essencielle, de noblesse en
France, c'est la vacation militaire.
— MONTAIGNE (1580)

Les marchans, les juges de villages, les artisans, nous les
voyons aller à pair de vaillance et science militaire aveq
la noblesse: ils rendent des combats honorables, et publiques et privez, ils battent, ils defendent villes en nos
guerres.
— MONTAIGNE (marginal addition after 1588)

I

Although rather tenuous at times, the special exemptions of
the nobility were not without their rationalization. They were
defended as necessary to preserve a superior racial strain (by
encouraging intermarriage among noble families), or to compensate the nobles for refraining from commerce. But by far
the most common argument was that the exemptions were
compensation for military service and for sacrifice in defense
of the state. Based on the traditional image of the nobility as
a knightly class, it was one of the oldest and simplest explanations of noble privilege. It had become one of the common-
places of the sixteenth century. "The true profession of the
nobility and the one which is most useful to the people and
the king," said the Venetian ambassador in a report about
France, "is that of warfare."[1] In the Estates General of 1576,
all three orders reaffirmed that the principal duty of the nobility was to defend the kingdom.[2] "The proper and only and
essential place for the nobility in France," said Montaigne,
"is the military profession."[3] That military service was a sufficient reason for privileged status seemed obvious. It was "certainly very reasonable," as Charles Loyseau expressed the ac-

cepted view, "that those who contributed their life for the defense of the state be exempted from contributing their possessions."[4]

But to some this basic explanation of noble privilege seemed less than convincing. It rested on the tacit assumptions that there was a special military class and that the nobility was this class. This may once have been true, at least true enough to make the argument plausible, but the situation had altered by the late sixteenth century. Were the nobles actually giving more military service than non-nobles? Were they a military class in any meaningful sense? As contemporaries considered these potentially explosive questions, they do not seem to have based their opinions on any thorough quantitative analysis of the military structure. But they were aware of three broad trends that were relevant to the military rationale of noble privilege: the declining use of the ban et arrière-ban, the growing importance of the infantry, and the breakdown of class segregation in military units.

The decline of the ban et arrière-ban, by which vassals had traditionally paid military service to their suzerain, is particularly significant, for it was supposedly here that nobles had the opportunity to respond as a class, to show that they were the fighting force par excellence.[5] Having ceased to be an important military arm during the closing phase of the Hundred Years' War, the ban et arrière-ban had since suffered constant deterioration of its prestige. As an inevitable result of the large-scale land transfers between 1450 and 1550, it had come to include a good many roturiers (non-nobles). Attempts were made to keep it aristocratic, at first by letting roturiers off with a financial payment, and then, since some roturiers insisted on appearing in person, by segregating the two orders at the muster. But these attempts had broken down. Nobles, too, were able to avoid serving personally by making a financial payment or hiring a substitute, and many did so. Others evaded their obligations by neither paying nor serving.[6] Those nobles who did serve in person were generally poor country nobles who had been unable to pay the redemption fee. Few in numbers, badly equipped, and poorly trained, they were ridiculed as a ragtag assemblage without military importance.[7]

By the middle of the sixteenth century, the ban et arrière-ban was nearly dead. In 1553, at one of its few general convocations, only 2,000 men, not all of whom were nobles, appeared. Henry II declared in disgust that this was not one-sixth of the service yielded by the institution in the past.[8] In 1574, a report from Languedoc described its degeneration in that province: whereas in the past several hundred well-armed, well-mounted men would answer the call, at present the poorest nobleman had more self-esteem than to respond.[9] And it was apparently the situation in Brittany that Noël Du Fail was describing when he said that in the past there had been large numbers of well-armed men, and "nobles of race" had been separated from anoblis, but now most nobles merely sent their valets and the whole thing was not up to much.[10]

Toward the end of the century, the institution was ridiculed by the Third Estate of Dauphiny as being of "no service or profit," for by the time it was decided to convoke the ban et arrière-ban (a matter on which there was often controversy), the time required for collecting financial payments from those who would not serve personally and choosing those who would serve was so great that it was already too late to do any good anyway. "His Majesty has seen how much assistance the nobles of Dauphiny have provided," the Third Estate continued. "When he called upon them by means of the arrière-ban, they paid him with words."[11]

By the late sixteenth century the ban et arrière-ban included very few nobles, and most of those who owed the service paid money instead.[12] The dilapidated institution was not even considered worth convoking for its military service by Henry IV, although he did call it up in order to collect the financial payment. What is clear, to say the least, is that the great majority of nobles no longer raised a finger in this most characteristically feudal and aristocratic form of military service.[13] Given this situation, the nobility as a whole could no longer be described as a warrior class, even in the limited way that they might have been earlier. This is significant, but it may be more important to inquire to what extent those nobles who did fight dominated the military force. For even though the majority of them did not enter the military vocation, those who did so might have been sufficiently numerous to comprise the majority of actual fighting men.

But however true this might have been at an earlier time, a shift in the relative importance of infantry and cavalry had a far-reaching effect on the social complexion of the fighting forces by the late sixteenth century. There had been infantry before, of course, and the bearing of arms by roturiers was not a new thing. In the past, however, roturiers had tended to be concentrated in a temporary, mercenary, and secondary foot soldiery alongside a dominant arm of mounted nobles. Even during the first half of the sixteenth century the infantry was composed mostly of Swiss and German mercenaries with some volunteer French units.[14] The organization of the army was rudimentary, and the mounted "ordnance companies" (special units of heavy cavalry) were still dominant. But there was no mistaking the trend. The infantry became more important as the cavalry declined, and particularly from the 1530's on, more French foot soldiers were used in preference to foreigners. In the army of 1552, according to one surviving roster, there were 13,500 German mercenaries; but they were outnumbered by the 18,700 French foot soldiers, very few of whom would have been nobles.[15]

It was not only through the rise of the infantry that roturiers were becoming militarily more conspicuous. Roturiers were also penetrating units that traditionally had been thought of as aristocratic. This had been true, as we have already pointed out, of the ban et arrière-ban. And it was true of the mounted ordnance companies, sometimes called the *gendarmerie*. When François de Veilleville took over the company at Lyons in 1547, he found a motley force of "innkeepers, sons of tavern-keepers, valets, house-porters, and tenant-farmers."[16] He expelled these roturiers, but there seems to have been no such program applied consistently in all such units. Infiltration was particularly heavy after the beginning of the civil wars, when ordnance companies were said to be composed mostly of roturiers and taillables.[17] In 1569, a foreign ambassador described them as being composed of "people of all kinds, even of very low condition."[18] And in 1583, when an effort was made to impose the taille on all roturiers who had illegally claimed exemptions, one of the groups designated was the roturiers of the ordnance companies.[19] Guy Coquille, a legist, was not far wrong when he remarked, in 1588, that non-nobles had taken over the gendarmerie.[20]

It is true that some of those who were joining these mounted companies were officeholders or anoblis who could hope to buttress their claim to full noble status by serving for a time in the military ranks. But the end result was to dilute or "bastardize" the traditionally noble service; the newcomers were denounced both for their pretensions to noble status and their inexperience.[21] A typical evaluation of the situation was that of a pamphleteer who composed a dialogue in which one character suggested that since the gendarmerie was composed largely of "new anoblis," any attempt to force them back into the *roture* would deprive the country of their military service. The other character in the dialogue responded as follows: "Are you of the opinion that the militia of France will be of much service when it is filled with persons of low estate, inexperienced and untrained in the use of arms? ... This is a manifest insult to our predecessors and to those gentlemen of noble and ancient race who have to act as the peers and companions of persons of lowly status and little value."[22] The domination of the ordnance companies by the nobility was, to say the least, something less than complete.

Even the positions of command were not inaccessible to roturiers. "When I first began to carry arms," said Blaise de

Monluc, "captain was a title of honor and it was not considered beneath gentlemen of good family.... Now the lowliest ox-team driver calls himself by this name."[23] I do not know of any statistical study of the military officers under Henry IV, and it may well be that nobles still held the majority of those positions. They did not, however, enjoy a monopoly.

At the same time that roturiers were serving in the ban et arrière-ban, the ordnance companies, and officers' posts, some nobles were serving in the lowly infantry, though it is unlikely that this was very widespread. A revealing incident late in the reign of Francis I was an attempt to allow foot service in lieu of ban et arrière-ban; the proposal roused little enthusiasm, and since it was obviously disastrous to the prestige of the institution it was soon abandoned.[24] The nobles had a congenital aversion to the infantry, which smacked too much of roture, and it was their refusal to serve in it, according to La Noue, that had "bastardized our infantry."[25] But their refusal was not total; there continued to be some nobles who did serve in the ranks of the infantry. In describing the levy of 1552, Vieilleville said that a great number of young nobles "who could not afford to come mounted" entered the infantry units.[26] Further, as the gendarmerie declined, the light cavalry or the infantry appeared to some young nobles as a more likely road to advancement.[27] Though the entrance of nobles into the infantry was not a large-scale movement, it reemphasizes what we have been noticing all along: the nobleman who fought for France in the late sixteenth century, in whatever branch and on whatever level, was likely to rub elbows with a goodly number of roturiers.

The failure of most nobles ever to perform military service and the increasing military importance of roturiers did not go unnoticed. Look well at both the mounted companies and the infantry, said an irate spokesman for the Third Estate in Dauphiny, and "scarcely one-thirtieth will be found to be nobles."[28] Another writer called attention to the distinctly unmartial character of the nobles, who, he said, had not demonstrated any enthusiasm for combat since an early battle of the religious wars in which they had suffered some casualties. Still, in order to continue their claim to be the military profession, they wore swords, thus "profiting from the convenience of war without suffering the inconveniences."[29] A similar observation was made in 1595 by the jurisconsults René Chopin and Estienne Pasquier: "The nobility flatters itself that the use of arms was given to it as its share, while to the people menial activities were given—just as though in all the wars of the past thirty-six years the common people had not contributed to this same [military] profession along with the nobility."[30]

It is significant that Chopin and Pasquier saw the breakdown of the nobility's special claim to the military profession as coinciding roughly with the religious wars. The large trends were already at work in the early part of the century, as we have seen, but it is probably true enough that the wars carried the process further and made it more noticeable. As armies were hurriedly organized, social distinctions often seemed less important than religion or faction. Large numbers of nonnoble mercenaries were relied upon. Although mounted warriors came back partly into their own during these wars, it was also then that roturiers slipped into cavalry units most easily. Thus the religious wars did not restore the nobility to its ancient role as a knightly class.

II

The military rationale of noble privilege obviously needed reexamining. Nobles continued to enjoy their privileges irrespective of whether they performed military service. Roturiers who served in the army, even as cavalry or as officers, were not elevated to noble status. For the military rationale to have become convincing again, the correlation between privilege and actual service would have had to be restored.

One way of accomplishing this would have been to require the nobility to bear its military responsibility directly, which there were some attempts to do. The movement to rejuvenate the ban et arrière-ban, for instance, often disclosed an impatience with the nobles' lack of ardor and a determination to make them earn their exemptions by actual service. The clergy, at the Estates General in 1560, demanded that nobles serve in person "unless they had a legitimate excuse."[31] In 1570, the Estates of Brittany pointed out that if nobles would serve in person the general cost of defense would be lessened, for nobles were exempt anyway and could do the job as well as the present hired soldiers.[32]

Others expressed stronger feelings. The Third Estate of Berry demanded in 1589 that nobles who evaded their military responsibilities be "deprived of the privileges of nobility and of their fiefs and jurisdictions."[33] It is doubtful that such views were stated in the interest of rationalizing the noble privileges; rather the mood seems to have been that since the nobles were privileged in return for military service, they should be forced to provide such service. Furthermore, the financial interest of the Third Estate was often a major consideration, as when spokesmen for the Third Estate demanded that the nobles, since they were not serving in the ban et arrière-ban anyway, be taxed for the payment of professional troops, and that the common people be relieved of this charge.[34] Whatever the underlying motive, the movement to force the nobles back into military service, or to a more satisfactory level of service, would have had the effect, had it succeeded, of reinforcing the traditional military rationale of privilege.

This was apparently recognized by at least some noblemen, for the demands were not expressed only by the Third Estate. All three orders of the *bailliage* of Loudun insisted with equal vigor that the nobles should serve personally.[35] François de La Noue was not the only nobleman to believe that restoring the ban et arrière-ban would do much for the nobility in the way of giving it a recognized function and disarming its critics.[36] Henry II tried to restore the ban et arrière-ban by requiring all those owing service under it "to serve us personally and actually."[37] In 1579, the Ordinance of Blois provided that nobles who failed to take arms as commanded would be deprived of both fiefs and noble status.[38] (A gloss of this passage by the jurist Nicolas Frerot explains that by virtue of having been granted fiefs, nobles were obliged "to serve the king and the crown in time of war, to expose their persons, their possessions, arms and horses, as the case may require."[39] According to a proclamation of 1589 nobles between the ages of twenty and sixty who refused to mount would not only lose their noble status but would be declared guilty of the crime of lèse-majesté. Similar royal edicts followed in 1591, 1593, 1595, and 1597.[40] The most respected jurists of the time agreed that failure of nobles to serve would entail loss of privileges, although they held differing opinions regarding the status of the children of degraded nobles. The movement, all in all, was an impressive one. If it had succeeded, the military rationale of noble privilege would have been rendered much more satisfying.

But these multiplying demands and ordinances requiring that nobles serve personally were not sufficient to reverse the long-range trend. The fact that the edicts had to be repeated year in and year out is a good indication that enforcement was not complete. In the 1620's, another effort to specify and enforce the requirements of personal service was exerted, but when this too failed, Richelieu was prompted to write of the ban et arrière-ban: "My conscience forces me to say boldly that recourse should never be had to such an aid; [it is] much more prejudicial than useful to the state."[41]

Some looked at the problem less strictly in terms of the ban et arrière-ban. Recognizing that with the rise of the infantry the nobility's importance in the entire military system had declined, they tried to discourage roturiers from entering all military ranks. There are 80,000 French nobles ready to ride, said one pamphleteer, and they could even be used in the infantry.[42] The nobles are better fighters, said another, and should be employed in the military enterprise.[43] Nicolas Pasquier (son of the famous Estienne Pasquier) urged that the ordnance companies be reorganized as in the past—i.e., as the dominant cavalry arm, made up entirely of noblemen.[44]

No one, I think, went so far as to advocate excluding roturiers entirely from the military service. But there was a feeling that they were only to be tolerated as a kind of unavoidable expediency, that they did not really belong, that they did not have innate military qualities—indeed, roturier soldiers were ridiculed as boorish peasants totally lacking in the qualities of fighting men. It was even advocated that foreign mercenaries rather than Frenchmen be employed as foot soldiers in order to assure the continued predominance of the nobility over the roturiers.*

But attempts to turn back the clock had little chance in the face of widespread recognition that roturier soldiers were here to stay. Moreover, along with ridicule, the ungentlemanly fighting man was frequently commended for his soldierly qualities. Brantôme wrote,

"What I admire especially in these foot soldiers is that young men from villages, shops, schools, smithies, and stables have no sooner lived for a time among the infantry than they are shaped, fashioned, and made warlike. From the nothing they were they rise to be captains equal to gentlemen, having as much honor and reputation as the most noble, and performing acts as virtuous and noble as the greatest of gentlemen."[45]

---

* An English traveler at the end of the century said of the French foot soldiers, "Being commonly the rascall sort, and such as have no other meanes, there cannot settle in their abiect mindes, that true and honourable resolution requisite in a souldier." Sir Robert Dallington, *The View of Fraunce, 1604* ([London], 1936), page M. Dickenson gives several examples of the disdain for roturier soldiers in *The "Instructions sur le faict de la guerre" of ...Fourquevaux* (London, 1954), p. xxviii.

In 1561, the Venetian ambassador declared that in France the cavalry was more important than the infantry: "The ready availability of Swiss and Germans, and the reluctance to arm peasants and the common people, have worked to the advantage of the cavalry, which is composed only of nobles." Tommaseo, ed., *Rélations des ambassadeurs vénetiens*, I, 491. The last phrase is an exaggeration, but the ambassador did notice a significant attitude toward extending arms to roturiers. See also V. G. Kiernan, "Foreign Mercenaries and Absolute Monarchy," *Past and Present*, XI (1957), 66–86, where the use of foreign mercenaries as an alternative to arming the people is seen as diverting danger from the old aristocratic order.

Monluc wrote that roturier soldiers were not only equal to nobles but often superior.[46] Montaigne, who observed roturier behavior in the religious wars, stated: "We see tradesmen, village justices, artisans, holding their own with the nobles in valour and military knowledge. They give a good account of themselves both in public battles and in private combats; they fight, they defend cities in our wars."[47] It was impossible to deny that many non-nobles were making material sacrifices, fighting with courage, and dying bravely in service of king and country.

It is not surprising, therefore, that some people began thinking of another way to restore the validity of the military rationale of privilege—namely, extend the traditional exemptions and privileges to roturier soldiers. In other words, rather than conform the military structure to the distribution of privilege, they would distribute privilege in accordance with actual military performance. There was a precedent: in 1448, the *francs-archers* (a newly created infantry arm) had been exempted from the taille, though not from other imposts. When the legion was created in 1534, roturier legionnaires were given a partial exemption of 20 sous per year. The exemptions do not seem to have been continued when the legion gave way to the regiment, about 1560, but it was only natural that the question would crop up again as part of the dialogue on the military rationale in the late sixteenth century.

Not that anyone intended to exempt every ordinary foot soldier and water boy; but there was a serious movement to exempt roturiers who had entered the ordnance companies. According to an edict of Charles IX, they were entitled to exemption from the taille after ten years' service. But this concession proved too generous in view of the large number of roturiers who were then entering the companies. Le Bret observed that if roturiers had been made exempt after ten years, "there would have been no one left to pay the taille."[48] This was apparently the opinion reflected in an ordinance of 1583 that declared the companies to be exempt but explicitly ex-

cluded those who were "taxable by nature."[49] A compromise
was finally worked out, in edicts of 1596 and 1600, which Le
Bret described in his discussion on the exemption of soldiers.
Some roturiers—those in the companies, or officers in the infantry—could gain exemption not after ten years' service but
after twenty. It was not made easy or automatic, however.
The king could confer the immunity on them "according as
their virtue merited it," which left some leeway; it was necessary after putting in the required number of years to obtain
certificates of nobility from the king and have them registered
by the Cour des Aides; and a single *acte dérogeant* (an act or
practice inconsistent with noble status), either during the
time of service or after the exemption was obtained, was dis-
qualifying. The exemption was not considered equivalent to
noble status, nor was it regarded as hereditary.[50]

Even this compromise solution was not entirely stable. Some
opposing interests and tensions can be discerned, for instance,
just a few years later, when an effort was made to return to
the severity of the 1583 ruling by totally excluding roturiers
from exemptions.[51] But the Cour des Aides mollified this effort by allowing exemptions to roturiers if they had served for
the required number of years and had not been guilty of degrading behavior.

One current of opinion—rather feeble but worth noting—
would not only have exempted roturier fighters but would
have ennobled them. Thus Brantôme considered that the profession of arms in itself ennobled the soldier, however humble
his birth.[52] It is difficult to know whether he was thinking of
actual noble status as legally defined or of a more ambiguous
nobility of virtue. Other writers clearly had legal status in
mind. In the Estates General of 1576, for instance, the clergy
suggested a program by which the young roturier could rise
in the social hierarchy. First he would serve as a simple soldier
for three years. Having passed this test, he could be made an
archer. Then after two years of good behavior as an archer
he would be eligible for promotion to *gendarme*. Finally,

after serving with distinction in this last capacity for fifteen years, and fighting valiantly in at least one battle, he would "acquire the status of nobility for himself and his posterity."[53] Since the whole process required twenty years, and was hedged with qualifications to ensure that promotion was by no means automatic, it could hardly be regarded as opening the floodgates. Along the same lines, if less specific, was the proposal of an anonymous nobleman in 1614 that "all simple soldiers might hope through military virtue to acquire the quality of nobility and to arrive at all the functions which are given and attributed to nobles."[54]

But the idea of making roturier soldiers into nobles was generally viewed unfavorably. Tiraqueau had grappled with the question and had concluded that while military service was endowed with special dignity, in itself it did not ennoble.[55] After the turn of the century, Thierriat carefully explained that exempting captains and gendarmes from the taille during their lifetime did not make them nobles. "If the gendarme and the captain were regarded as nobles," he said, "then libertines and scoundrels could be nobles."[56] This was the dominant view and the official attitude. Such proposals as that of the clergy in 1576, while anticipatory of later demands for a *noblesse militaire*, were as yet only an undercurrent.

III

What is perhaps most surprising is the equanimity with which the old military rationalization of privilege was repeated. Obviously many nobles were not soldiers; obviously nobles did not exercise the military function exclusively. Yet Montaigne could say, without any apparent sense of discrepancy, that it was the nobility's exclusive and essential characteristic. And he was not alone in repeating the traditional view without any suggestion of nuance or of changing conditions. To understand this, we have to remember that the transformation had been going on for a long time. Stereotypes are not easily discarded, especially when the public mind has time to adjust gradually to the changing conditions. Had the nobles completely abandoned the military profession, the stereotype could scarcely have been maintained, but they never actually became militarily insignificant. Although few of them entered the military ranks and although those few seem to have made up only a minority of the fighting force, the noble class comprised less than two percent of the population.* Its participation in the military function always remained above that of the population in general, which might entitle it to be considered as a military class, speaking relatively.[57]

As far as officer positions are concerned, we have noted that some roturiers were officers. Actually, however, it was not until about the beginning of the seventeenth century that something like an officer corps began to appear, as part of the "military revolution" that reached its culmination in the Thirty Years' War. Since the nobles could not seriously hope to monopolize the entire army, their great chance to reclaim and redefine their function was through domination of the officer corps. They never achieved a monopoly, of course, and at times roturier officers became very numerous; but by and large the nobles did succeed in dominating the officer corps numerically (even in 1750 two-thirds of the infantry officers were nobles), and psychologically they set the tone for the military profession. The mystical gap between officers and men, which has continued to characterize military hierarchies, quite clearly derived from a basic difference of social class. The nobility's tenacious hold on key positions of military command gave at least some plausibility to the military rationale of privilege.

Still, it cannot be said that the military rationale of noble privilege was adequately defended during our period. For one

---

* Estimates of the number of nobles in the sixteenth century are largely guesses. Georges Lefebvre estimated that in the eighteenth century there were not more than 400,000 nobles out of a population of 23 million. *The Coming of the French Revolution* (New York, 1957), p. 7. This is less than two percent of the population. The percentage of nobles would not have been higher in the sixteenth century and may have been lower.

thing, the efforts to maintain it in the face of criticism were sporadic and disorganized and often lacked consistency. Those who wanted to keep the roturiers out of the ordnance companies and those willing to extend exemptions to roturiers who entered the companies, for example, were working at cross-purposes. There were larger problems as well. All the time that efforts were being made to restore the nobility to its ancient domination of the military service, other efforts were directed, as we shall see in the next chapter, toward restoring it to public offices. Although not exactly contradictory, these two objectives required different types of preparation and at bottom represented different images of the function of the noble class. With such fundamental confusion, it is natural that questions were raised about the nobles' military importance, that they were ridiculed, that various proposals to restore the correlation between actual service and privilege were heard, and that to some the nobility began to appear as an obsolescent class, lacking a social function, and therefore lacking justification for its privileged treatment.

CHAPTER 3

Public Office

Or de ma part j'ay toujours naturellement desdaigné un
honneur acheté et un profit qui ne vient d'un honneste
merite.
—Louis Turquet de Mayerne (1611)

Apres avoir perdu la possession des charges et dignitez
de l'Eglise nous avons aussi laissé partir de nos mains
l'administration de la justice et ne sommes plus aujourd'huy que la proye de nos inferieurs.
—*Discours d'un gentilhomme françois* (1614)

I

It is becoming clear that the nobility was suffering not only
from declining income but also from confusion about its social
function. Demoralized for lack of a clear self-image, it was
groping for a recognized social role; obviously the justification of its privileges and exemptions was tied closely to the
question of its special function. In this situation it was natural
to think of the sphere of government, for if the nobles could
win control of the highest governmental posts, they would
profit both financially and psychologically. The effort to ac-
complish this, while not entirely consistent with simultaneous
efforts to refashion the nobility into a knightly class, was
nevertheless part of the same attempt to clarify and define its
proper social role.[1]

It would be a mistake, of course, to think of the nobility as
having lost all governing functions. At the end of the sixteenth
century, the *noblesse d'épée*, or nobles of the sword, still dominated the three large groups of courtiers: the *grands officiers*,
the Conseil du Roi, and the Maison du Roi. Also drawn from
the nobility were most of the ambassadors, the *baillis* and

sénéchaux, and the governors of provinces.* But the nobles had lost some positions as far back as the reign of Philip Augustus. More important, between about 1450 and 1550 they had suffered a drastic curtailment of their traditional rights of seigneurial justice.[2] Many municipal offices previously held by noblemen were lost to town dwellers during the same period.[3] And as the number of sovereign courts multiplied, most of the judges and councillors were drawn from outside the old nobility.[4] The proliferation of venal offices, one of the striking features of the sixteenth century, was almost entirely to the advantage of non-nobles. Admittedly, many of these new officials eventually tried to claim noble status, but the old nobility had a strong sense of being dispossessed of its public functions.

There had been complaints about the loss of positions early in the sixteenth century, as for example by Claude de Seyssel, who first published *La grande monarchie de France* in 1515. But in the late sixteenth century, when several trends converged to produce an enormous class malaise, there was real consternation. Monluc lamented the nobles' having let the municipal offices fall to townsmen so that "we have to bow and scrape before them."[5] The nobles of Dauphiny were equally nettled but admitted that they had defaulted by retiring "to live in a certain idleness in the country."[6] For Du Haillan, who was thinking primarily of the Parlements, the underlying cause of the problem was the practice of selling offices. The nobles, "not wishing to chicane or to buy that which is the due of virtue," had simply abandoned the parliamentary positions.†

* Even in these offices there had been some incursions of what Doucet calls "gens de robe, prenant le pas sur les gentilshommes." *Les institutions de la France au XVIe siècle,* I, 139. For the displacement of nobles by roturiers in the Conseil du Roi, see Noël Valois, *Le Conseil du Roi aux XIVe, XVe, et XVIe siècles* (Paris, 1888), pp. 162–63, 172, 177.

† Du Haillan, *De l'estat et succez des affaires de France,* rev. ed. (n.p., 1611), pp. 173–74. It may be indicative of the growing concern with the nobility's displacement that the passage quoted did not appear in the original 1570 edition of the work but was added in the revised edition.

In 1567, an anonymous writer complained that Catherine de Médicis gave preference to commoners in filling positions at court. Is it not shameful, he asked, to see around the king the son of a notary, the son of a *procureur,* and a commissioner of supplies, who mixes with all sorts of menial and lowly persons? Considering roturiers easier to manage than nobles, the rulers had since 1559 "abased the ones and raised up the others, making of the noble a villein and of the villein a noble, certainly a transubstantiation of contrary honors." Was this practice not ruining the nobility, by taking away its income?[7] The gentleman apparently was thinking primarily of the pensions and perquisites of the royal court. An answering pamphlet of the same year viewed the question in larger perspective: "When all is said, it would not be possible to ruin [the nobility] more easily than by rendering it useless, which is what will happen if it is not employed. For what is not employed is useless, and what is useless is despised by all."[8] While blaming the foreign influence at court, this observer did not absolve the nobility from all responsibility. In recent years, he said, its performance had not been impressive. If it would show what it could do, proving its usefulness, the king would surely arrange things as before.

These two pamphlets of the 1560's raised a problem that would be wrestled with time and time again during the next two or three generations. Rather than merely urging the return of the nobles to prominence, the first gentleman had asked the king to "reestablish a government under which leading and virtuous men will be honored and recompensed according to their merits"—making a gratuitous assumption that the nobility had been displaced not by ability but by wealth and that the nobility would benefit if offices were granted on the basis of merit.[9] The issue, in other words, was posed in terms of "merit" and "virtue" as opposed to "venality"—favorite catchwords of the prolonged discussion that followed.

If the premise were accepted that merit and not venality should be the decisive factor in appointments to public offices, there were three broad positions that those favoring the elevation of the nobility to supremacy in government could adopt. The first was to maintain that only the nobility possessed sufficient merit, or that the nobility was uniquely qualified, for the desired posts. This seems to have been the attitude of the two anonymous pamphleteers of 1567. Others also asserted that using merit as the sole criterion of advancement would inevitably favor the nobles. In 1574, for instance, Eymar de Froydeville declared that if things were arranged "by geometric proportion, which is to say by individual merit, and not by arithmetic proportion, which is to say by amount of gold or silver, all would see that the virtuous and noble would stand out above the foolish."[10] In 1603, Pierre de Boyssat, of Dauphiny, wrote that the most perfect government was that of a king served by his nobility. The necessary virtue and merit, it said, "cannot be found in plebeians, because manual labor and the exercise of trades and physical work" have deprived them of such "qualities of mind."[11]

In the 1610's, Nicolas Pasquier wrote a letter to the king complaining about the nobility's treatment. There was a time, he said, when nobles could look to be rewarded for their services by an appointment of some kind. But now that all offices were venal, what could a young gentleman hope for? Positions should be assigned on the basis of merit and not of wealth. The assumption was, of course, that the nobles would most readily qualify if judged by the criterion of merit.[12]

But it was not easy to accept such a facile conclusion, and those who desired both to bestow offices on the nobility and to recognize individual merit had to determine what should be done if the two qualities did not coincide. In 1561, Pierre de La Place had urged that preference be given to nobles even if they had not particularly distinguished themselves; this he felt to be justified by the past and anticipated future excellence of the noble family. And yet even he would not completely ignore the question of merit; noble status, he observed, cannot remove the "impediment of human stupidity."[13]

In some ways this view foreshadowed that of Jean Bodin, who dealt with the question at length in his famous *Republic*. The idea of granting estates and offices only to those who deserved them was all very high sounding, he said, but this would keep the state in continual ferment. Men of the necessary ability were "very few and could easily be driven out and overcome by the others."[14] Of course it would be preferable to limit positions of responsibility to the deserving, but Bodin considered this impossible. The necessary qualities were not common enough. What Bodin came to regard as the only feasible solution was a compromise: to place the meritorious in positions whenever possible, but to grant public charges also on the bases of wealth and nobility. There would of necessity be some positions granted to rich or noble persons who were unworthy and incapable, but they should be kept to a minimum and should be those in which the least harm could be done. Perhaps, Bodin suggested, such a "mixture" could even have a certain salutary effect. The nobility would rejoice "to see the sole fact of noble status recognized in the distribution of charges"; and roturiers would be "thrilled beyond belief" to find themselves on the same level as the aristocracy.[15]

Bodin's was a realistic compromise, but there was a third approach, which was to become increasingly popular among people mainly interested in a secure and acknowledged function for the nobles. This, in brief, was to allow that offices should be granted on the basis of merit, but then to urge the nobles to qualify themselves, so that even on these grounds they might compete successfully. Perhaps an inevitable consequence of the desire both to reward merit and to elevate the nobility, this approach seemed all the more necessary in view of the appalling educational deficiencies of most nobles as against the increased need for professional legal training.

It is not surprising that most nobles found themselves unequipped for the magistracy, and for other positions as well. Their military and anti-intellectual traditions aside, legal education was a long process; preliminary studies of French, Latin, and Greek were followed by an arduous program of studies at the university. At the same time, laws and commentaries were becoming more numerous and more complex. The helplessness of the non-professional in this situation is illustrated by an interesting lawsuit at the beginning of the seventeenth century. A certain Pierre Billard was claiming the position of Lieutenant-Criminel de Robe Courte in Bourbonnais, a position that had been established in 1554. He was told that the position had been abolished in 1564; but what interests us more is the complaint that Billard lacked "knowledge and experience in legal matters." He was, it was said, "ignorant of the laws and ordinances and usages of the kingdom. In fact, it has been only in the past two or three years that he even learned how to read and barely to sign his name. How then can he judge matters of honor and of human life?"[16] The same question could have been raised about many nobles. Their boorishness was notorious, giving rise to the frequent charge that they had disqualified themselves by illiteracy, backwardness, and general incompetence. "The non-nobles did not take the judicial posts from us," said Tavannes; "it is ignorance that keeps them from us."[17] Later, the Englishman Sir Robert Dallington observed that the French nobility was without employment "for lack of instruction." Many other contemporaries agreed.[18]

If this diagnosis was sound, some nobles reasoned, the solution to their problem was obvious: they must become educated. "The door is open," said Tavannes, "to all those who see to the education of their children."[19] There were other reasons too, of course, for nobles to educate themselves. One writer urged them to learn letters in order that they might immortalize the deeds of their ancestors through written histories.[20] Some moralists regarded learning as an avenue to wisdom or as a means of reforming behavior.[21] But whatever other motives might have operated, the various proposals for educating the nobles were closely linked to their desire to regain domination of the public functions.

II

Having become familiar with the nobility's need to establish for itself a recognized social function, the loss of its public positions, and the basic dilemmas regarding merit and education, we are in a position to consider some of the contemporary treatises and pamphlets that dealt with the problem. In 1577, François de L'Alouëte, an experienced lawyer and official, brought out a treatise that dealt largely with the nobility. After observing that in power and wealth the nobility was a mere shadow of its former self, he put his finger on what he considered the most basic cause: the loss of public positions.[22] The fault for this state of affairs he placed squarely on the nobles themsleves, who, preferring pleasure, vanity, and ignorance, had rendered themselves unworthy of responsibility and had abandoned "the public work for their individual profit."[23] Their lack of learning, he continued, had been all the more damaging in that the laws had become so complicated that one now had to be well trained in jurisprudence in order to understand them.[24] Furthermore it used to be that nobles could exercise both arms and public functions; but now these had become two separate vocations.

L'Alouëte's prescription for restoring the nobility did not consist of education alone—he also urged a simplification of the laws so that "the noble of mediocre education could render justice without too much difficulty."[25] And he wanted the line between nobles and roturiers clarified by the careful preparation of family records.[26] Nevertheless, his program centered on the proposal that the king should honor the nobles by giving them positions, and that they should prove worthy of such treatment by their virtue and their education.

The next year, a thin duodecimo by Pierre d'Origny was published. Though given over mostly to lofty generalizations

about virtue and honor, it did make one specific suggestion:
a special academy should be established for young nobles.[27] It
was to be an institution "marvelously large and spacious," in
which the children of noblemen could be given a broad education until they reached the age of eighteen. Then, following "the inclination of their nature," they could choose a profession. Those going into theology, law, or medicine would
remain for six more years of advanced instruction. Those of
a military bent would undergo four years of field training. It
must be allowed that preparing the nobles for public positions
was not the major consideration in Origny's mind. He argued,
perhaps for the benefit of the king, that such professional military training would in less than six years provide five or six
thousand trained leaders for the royal army.[28] Nevertheless,
Origny appreciated the necessity of educating the nobles if
they were to advance into positions of responsibility. When a
bishopric became available, he explained, a noble theologian
could fill it if there were nobles in the divinity schools. Likewise, a judicial post could be filled by a trained noble jurist;
and if the nobles were trained in languages, they could more
easily be selected as ambassadors. The whole program was calculated, therefore, not only to benefit the state, but also to provide for the "relief of the poor nobles."

There were others who were urging education as the solution to the nobility's problems. David Du Rivault, for instance,
attacked the old bromide that learning was unaristocratic and
demeaning. The Greek and Roman nobles were proficient in
both arms and letters, he said, and their decline came only
when they neglected either the one or the other; unfortunately the nobility of the present "so despises the enrichment
of the mind" that "nothing seems to it more vile and less esti-
mable."[29] About the same time, another writer argued that
since ignorance of letters made the nobles incapable of serving
the state in time of peace, they had no right to complain if
"the capacity of someone lesser is preferred."[30]

In 1606 Florentin de Thierriat's massive *Trois traités* ap-

peared. The public function's having largely passed to non-
nobles Thierriat explained as being due primarily to the nobility's lack of education: "The calamity of the time and the
ignorance that we affect have brought us to the point of not
being preferred to roturiers unless equal to them in merit. It
is judged unreasonable that a gentleman destitute of knowledge and experience be preferred to an experienced and
learned roturier."[31] As a matter of abstract principle, Thierriat believed that nobles should occupy the places of public
responsibility. This had been the practice among the Jews, the
Greeks, and the Romans. It was also reasonable, he thought,
since those who were "truly noble" were more determined to
fill their posts with honor and distinction.[32] One class of positions, ambassadorships, he thought should be reserved for
nobles simply because nobles would be better received by foreign princes.[33]

But Thierriat's desire to aid the nobility did not blind him
to the importance of merit. The king, he said, would have to
choose nobles known to be upright, for it was hazardous to
assign responsibilities on the basis of noble status "without
some other proof of virtue and fidelity."[34] In cases of hard
choice Thierriat would give the nod to the nobleman—but
only if all other things were equal.[35] Thus, although not stated
quite so starkly as elsewhere, the main hope of the nobility
again seemed to lie in education, which Thierriat praised and
recommended at some length.

During the disorderly decade that followed the assassina-
tion of Henry IV, discussion of the nobility's public role continued. In 1611, an audacious work by Louis Turquet de Mayerne announced in the preface, "For my part I have always
despised a purchased honor or a profit that does not come
from honest merit."[36] Merit was to be the passport to recognition and advancement. The principle could be applied to the
social hierarchy in general, with the hereditary aristocracy being recast into a genuine elite.[37] It also had implications for

the question of employing nobles in public positions. For Mayerne, performance was the thing. Nobles should prove their worth not only as soldiers but also as administrators, judges, scholars, artists, farmers, physicians, and tradesmen.[38] He did see a place for nobles in the government; he went so far as to stipulate that each Parlement should include some members from the old nobility ("de robe courte"). But never should a person, whatever his social class, be appointed or promoted except on the basis of merit. If nobles were free to enter public service, so was everyone else; all would compete on equal grounds.

It is possible, as some had contended, that exclusive reliance on merit as a criterion for advancement would have been to the nobility's advantage. But this was not the opinion of Mayerne, who did not regard the nobility as possessing any inherent superiority of talent or ability. Virtue, he thought, was "not restricted to any one social class," but was "divided by the Moderator of the universe among nobles and roturiers, strong and weak, and among the poor as among the rich." We should not, he warned, consider only the things that are considered by "the common herd, who give all their attention to nobility of race, to some general appearance of valor, or to riches that can be seen." If followed, Mayerne's program would have resulted in a colossal social upheaval. It is a truism that he was in advance of his time. But when *La monarchie aristodémocratique* is placed among the works we have been discussing in this chapter, there is little in its argument that had not been formulated before, or that had not been implicit in the demands that advancement be determined by merit. Indeed, Mayerne simply carried the premise to its logical conclusion.

The whole question of the nobility's role in government became a matter of lively controversy during the Estates General of 1614. The flood of pamphlets that appeared before and during that meeting touched upon many different problems, ranging all the way from the mechanics of election to broad descriptions of the woes of France. It was natural that the question of the nobility's proper place in public life should again be raised.

In 1614, or possibly slightly earlier, an anonymous work entitled *Le paysan françois* was published.[39] Its author was a firm advocate of installing the nobles of France in leading public positions. The advantages of such a policy, he said, would be several. The nobility would be relieved of its poverty and would become "rich and opulent." This would be no small relief to the king, who then would not be constantly importuned for pensions by poor nobles. Moreover, in the public positions the nobility would do a better job; having "more heart" than roturiers, they would administer the charges "more nobly and more virtuously."[40] Nobles should not only be allowed to apply for the public positions, therefore, but they should be actively sought out and "invited."[41]

This pamphlet appears to be in the tradition of the proponents of education as the avenue to preferment. It too blamed lack of education for the fact that the nobility had been forced to abandon the public charges "almost entirely."[42] Also, its author spared no pains to refute the tired claim that education and letters would make young gentlemen cowardly and effeminate and wholly incapable of bearing arms. Education, he reasoned, would not make nobles courageous if they were not so already, but neither would it make them more timid and cowardly than they naturally were. Education might make bad men worse, he conceded, but it should not hurt the "strong and generous natures of the nobility."[43]

Nevertheless, there are certain limitations in the outlook of this work. Merit was not really considered as part of the problem, thus excluding rather arbitrarily the one question that had always in the past prevented easy solutions. Nor was there any evidence of a desire to provide the nobility with a useful social function. What this author had in mind, if we examine his description closely, was not functional positions at all but venal offices, usually considered rather as investment or property than as opportunities for service. For example, he insisted that the nobleman could hold public charges and at the same time continue his military duties because some of the civil offices were held alternately, by semester.[44] The emphasis was decidedly not on fulfilling the responsibilities of public service, but on the profits, the *épices*, which the nobles would be able to enjoy. Any doubts as to the type of public positions he had in mind for the nobility are removed if we examine the conclusion to his statement that lack of education originally had led the nobles to abandon posts of public responsibility. Now, he said, the situation was entirely changed; learning was no longer a prerequisite. One could be as diligent as a Budé (who was said to have studied for seven hours on his wedding day), as resolute as a Bartolus, as profound as a Du Moulin, as learned as a Cujas—but without money he would not procure an office.[45] It was such offices, venal and superfluous, that the author of *Le paysan françois* apparently wished to bestow on the nobility.

His intent became still clearer when he explained how his proposal would help to solve the problem of too many office-holders, that chronic source of complaint. Both nobles and officiers, he said, could be considered as "vocations onereuses," which means, one would gather from the context, that these were not necessary functions for which a salary or some kind of commensurate reward was returned, but were rather arbitrary and nonfunctional honors the expense of which fell upon the people. To combine them by giving the offices to the nobles would therefore have the advantage of greatly decreasing the total burden. It would be "a remedy of sorts."[46] Such a line of reasoning had enormous possibilities. Indirectly, it was an attack on the nobility as parasitical; it could be inferred that officiers and nobles were equally undesirable, to be decreased in numbers immediately and eradicated as soon as possible. But this conclusion was not made explicit. As it stands, *Le paysan françois* was an appeal to return the nobles to public offices—but with a difference. Merit, education, service, responsibility, those great key words of most of the works we have been considering, were either missing entirely or distorted beyond recognition.

Another pamphlet printed in 1614 purported to be by six peasants.[47] Among its demands was the restoration of the nobility "to its original splendor" by grants of certain positions. Yet when we see what positions were to be reserved for the nobility, the proposal loses much of its apparent vigor. The members of the Maison du Roi, the gendarmes, the chancellor, the councillors of state, all these were to be nobles, but on one condition: that "the other gentlemen, those of the Third Estate" could also receive appointments when they excelled in virtue and capacity.[48] It was also proposed that nobles be preferred in appointments to judgeships. But here too there was the condition: "The door will always be open for virtue, whatever one's social class."[49]

It is tempting to regard this pamphlet as simply a manifestation of class antagonism, an attempt to exclude the nobles from any worthwhile participation in public affairs. A more judicious interpretation, I believe, would recognize that its authors, like many of their contemporaries, were willing to see the nobles fill a niche within the state. But this desire was at once too restricted and too vague to result in any genuine improvement. Above all, it was impeded by the opposing principle of merit, which, almost as an afterthought, always seemed to assert itself. This principle had persistently refused to be reconciled with the idea of favoring certain persons simply because they had been born into noble families. In a broad sense, therefore, the pamphlet was typical, representing the cul-de-sac into which the whole question of nobles in public office had worked itself.

As might be expected, the nobles too had views on the subject of their proper role in the state. The question came up in their discussions and it entered into their cahiers. It was also prominent in a remarkable pamphlet by an anonymous nobleman, the *Discours d'un gentilhomme françois à la noblesse de*

France.[50] The chief affliction of France in general and the nobility in particular, said the author, was venality. It was "the first cause of the ruin and decadence of this flourishing kingdom and of the bastardization of the nobility."[51] At one time, he continued, the nobility possessed all of the principal offices of the kingdom, both in the judiciary and in the church, which were never granted to a roturier unless by his virtue, probity, and capacity he showed himself "worthy to be associated with the nobles." Then, in the course of time, the nobles of France lost both church dignities and the administration of justice, until they had come to be at the mercy of their inferiors.[52] The *Discours* did not trace this decline in detail, but it did assert that the main obstacle to a return of nobles to public life was venality: "True gentlemen can no longer hope to arrive at any charge by reason of either birth or merit; but the children of the officiers of justice and finance, with their relatives or their connections, can hope to possess everything, since they have money in their hands."[53]

Where the *Discours* went beyond most other contemporary discussions of the problem was in its demand that the nobility be given a virtual monopoly, not only of such traditional posts as ambassador, bailli, and the charges of the Maison du Roi, but also of all positions of any importance in the sovereign courts.[54] It had been suggested by others that one-third of the councillors of the Parlements should be nobles of race. But the *Discours* urged the appointment of nobles not only as the presidents of Parlement, the Cours des Aides, and the Chambre des Comptes but also as councillors, *avocats*, and procureurs of the same courts; and as *maistres* and *correcteurs* of the Chambre des Comptes. The auditors of the Chambre des Comptes, while remaining legally non-noble, would be exempted from payment of the taille, and if they served faithfully for many years, or died in office, their children would be declared nobles of the second generation.[55] Interestingly enough, the author's reluctance to extend the nobility's domination further into the financial department had nothing to do with the supposed incompatibility of such activities with noble status; he argued rather that the king would be better served if the powers of justice and finance were separated and that the hope of eventual ennoblement could serve to increase the zeal of his financial officers.

Despite the author's complaints about merit no longer being rewarded, it must not be assumed that he advocated using it as the only criterion for advancement. Occasional "hommes rares" might be allowed entrance into the aristocratic circle. But that this was scarcely a magnanimous concession is clearly indicated by the example he gave: if a roturier served with distinction as an avocat for at least ten years, he then might be given the position of councillor in one of the courts.[56] Nor was the author so lofty in his perspective that he ignored the nobility's financial needs; the pecuniary motive was still in evidence, particularly with respect to the pensions of the royal court.*

III

The pamphlets and treatises indicate that there was sustained interest in improving the nobility's performance in public functions. But the advocates of giving more public responsibility to nobles had to find more effective ways of making their views known. An ideal platform for this purpose was the Estates General, which enjoyed a brief revival of sorts between 1560 and 1614. Among the many demands presented there, it is not surprising to find the noble delegates demanding a more generous share of public offices. The general cahiers of the Second Estate (which attempted to represent the desires of the nobility as a whole) can be conveniently approached by con-

---

* Pensions and sinecures should be granted to the leading and "most virtuous" members of the nobility in order to provide them with the means of serving His Majesty "in war as in peace," and to "repay them for the loss of blood and the expenditures that they have made for the support of the state during the recent wars." Anon., *Discours d'un gentilhomme françois à la noblesse de France,* p. 23.

sidering their demands in each of three broad areas of government.

1. *The royal court.* Without expressly stipulating that only nobles be admitted to the court, the cahiers of 1560 gave evidence of a desire to increase the number of available openings in the Maison du Roi, the Maison de la Reine, etc., by putting a stop to the practice of allowing a person to hold more than one position. By all indications, the motive of the nobles here was strictly pecuniary—to provide some reward for loyal, worthy, and deserving persons.[57] Going beyond the attack on pluralism, the nobility in 1576 demanded that only noblemen "de nom et d'armes" be employed in the Chambre du Roi, the Maison du Roi, the Compagnie de Cent Gentilshommes, and in ambassadorships, and that any non-nobles then in such positions be promptly discharged.[58] Similar requests were made in 1588 and in 1614.[59]

As to the royal councils and the *grands offices* (chancellor, constable, admiral, and others), nothing specific was demanded in 1560, although they may have been included among the "grand offices" that the deputies wished to have given to the French nobility rather than to foreigners.[60] It is perhaps indicative of the growing tensions that the cahiers of 1576 did specify that the chancellor and the secretaries of state be chosen from among the nobility, and that all present members of the Conseil Privé be discharged.[61] The Conseil would then be reorganized with eighteen councillors, six of whom would be "de longue robe catholique" and twelve "gentilshommes d'honneur."[62]

2. *The sovereign courts.* In 1560, all three cahiers of the Second Estate agreed that a place should be made for nobles in the sovereign courts—Parlements, Chambre des Comptes, Cours des Aides, etc.—which were now "filled by the third and common estate."[63] In fact, one-third of the councillorships were claimed "for the protection of the rights of nobles."[64] This demand was repeated with emphasis in 1576: four of the

twelve councillors of the Parlements should be nobles "de robe courte portans épées."[65] Similar statements are in the cahiers of 1588 and 1614.[66]

Also of interest to the nobles were the subordinate offices connected with the courts, the so-called *offices de judicature.* The main proposal in 1560 was to regulate the method of filling vacancies so that the nobles would have a better chance of winning appointments. The method traditionally followed was called "pricking": the court itself would name some acceptable candidates, usually three, for a vacant office, and the king would then make his selection from this list. Without completely repudiating this custom, the cahiers of 1560 proposed to modify it: sale of offices would be strictly forbidden, and the nobility would be allowed some voice in choosing the candidates. As expressed by the second cahier of the nobles, the list of candidates presented to the king should contain the names of three persons of substance ("personnes suffisantes") —"or, if there be capable noblemen, let them be named first, to the end that at least one-third of the offices of justice will be of the noble class."[67] The same demands were heard in 1588 and in 1614. The nobility wished to render to the king "as much testimony of its fidelity in the exercise of justice as it does in the armies." It was hoped that they could "fill the sovereign courts with the gentlemen who composed them in ancient times."[68]

3. *Local and provincial administration.* The demand heard most frequently here was that baillis and sénéchaux be noblemen "du pays et de courte robe,"[69] which meant not only that roturiers should be replaced by nobles, but also that absenteeism should be discontinued. Since the demand to reserve these posts for nobles was often repeated, it is clear that they were the focus of the nobility's ambition in the area of local and provincial administration. In view of the declining importance of these offices, however, it is interesting to know that at the Assembly of Notables in 1597 the noble delegates expressed a desire for the position of *lieutenants de bailliage*

also, and in 1614 they wished to reserve for noblemen the position of consul or mayor in the towns.

It is clear enough that the nobles felt dispossessed, that they had lost practically all their posts with the sovereign courts, and that they were being displaced even as baillis and sénéchaux. Otherwise the demands—for example, that at least one-third of the councillors of the Parlements be nobles—would make no sense.*

It would not be correct to say that these demands were entirely ignored. Some concessions were made by Henry III. Henry IV, in particular, made an effort to give the nobles a greater share in government.[70] Even the proposals for improving noble education were not entirely fruitless. In Languedoc, for example, the Estates put aside a certain sum "for an Academy that the Estates desire to be established for the instruction of the nobility."[71] But all in all the gains were not impressive. The positions set aside for the nobility were mostly military or largely formal—some posts at court, the declining position of bailli, ambassadorships, and some military captaincies. They were few in comparison both to the total number of offices and to the overall needs of the nobility. The responses of the kings to the demands expressed in the cahiers—in 1560, 1576, 1588, and 1614—were either evasive ("Le roi y advisera") or equivocal (it will be "very easy to gratify the nobles providing they have the other required qualities"). And none of these rulers showed enthusiasm for the nobility's judicial ambitions.

In a sense, the government was taking away with one hand what it was offering with the other. In 1604, the famous edict of La Paulette regulated the sale of offices; if it did not exactly make all offices hereditary, it did have the effect of accelerat-

---

* It is not helpful to cite examples of *noblesse de robe* in support of the argument that the nobles still occupied many positions. Their status was ambiguous, as we shall see in Chapter 6, and in any case they were regarded by the old noble families as aliens. The full-scale merger of the two aristocracies was still in the future.

ing and legalizing the existing tendency for the venal offices to be hereditary. There were attacks on La Paulette, of course, as there continued to be on the practice of venality, but they were not successful.[72]

That the nobles were not achieving their objectives was becoming obvious. Despite all the efforts of the preceding decades, and the apparent concessions, they seemed to be about where they were in 1560. The demand that only nobles be chosen as baillis and sénéchaux, for instance, had been readily granted by the king; yet it had had to be repeated in 1560, 1576, 1588, and 1614. In 1615, over two hundred noblemen appeared before the chancellor to complain that the positions at court were still being sold and that the nobles were not being favored. "In short," they grumbled, "you treat us more barbarously than *à la Turque*, making no distinctions according to order, extraction, or merit."[73] The same year, a small anonymous work appeared under the title *Avis au roi pour faire entrer la noblesse et gens de mérite aux charges.** It was reissued in 1617. The idea of favoring nobles in the distribution of public offices was still very much in the air, and it could still be coupled, as the title indicates, with the assumption that merit and nobility went hand in hand.

One of the delegates from the clergy at the Estates General of 1614 was Richelieu. Since his voice would be of commanding importance within ten years, a brief examination of his views on the question of the nobility and public offices may conveniently show how far things had progressed, or failed to progress, between 1614 and 1640. A member of the lesser nobility himself, Richelieu was not unsympathetic to the nobility's desires. An ordinance prepared by him almost imme-

---

* The full title is *Avis au roi pour faire entrer la noblesse et gens de mérite aux charges, & pourvoir au prix excessif des offices, sans mescontenter les officiers* (Paris, 1615). The essence of the argument was that if the price of offices were lowered, "la noblesse, & les personnes de mérite & de scavoir pourroyent facilement entrer aux charges sans s'incommoder." The favoring of the nobles, which was not the major objective of the scheme, would come after the general lowering of office prices. Pp. 9–10.

diately after he became first minister (an ordinance that was never applied) provided that certain posts in the reorganized upper councils be reserved for nobles of the sword. When the nobles at the 1627 Assembly of Notables renewed the demands for specific offices and for special schools, he was sympathetic enough. He was anxious to find means, as he expressed it, to "give advantage to the nobility."

And yet Richelieu's conception of the role of nobility in government, quite aside from the practical obstacles in the way of his program, was not, from the nobles' point of view, everything that could be desired. Their role in public affairs was to be a strictly limited one, with the military responsibility remaining primary. The posts that he urged the king to assign to nobles—governorships, captaincies, and membership in the Maison du Roi—were military or formal, and they were far from satisfying the specific demands that had been made, for instance, in 1614 and 1627. Even had he been more enthusiastic about returning political responsibilities to the nobility, there were practical obstacles that could not be overcome. His desire to found an academy for five hundred young noblemen, for instance, was frustrated by the lack of money. Indeed, there is pathos in his concluding remarks on the nobility in the *Testament politique*: "Many other things could be proposed for the relief of the nobility. But I smother all such thoughts, realizing that, as easy as they would be to write down, they would be very difficult and perhaps impossible to realize in practice."[74]

The ambivalence of Richelieu's stand—desiring to favor the nobility, yet restricted in the extent of his aims and in his ability to implement them—helps to explain the mixture of hope and despair in a pamphlet addressed to him in 1634 by a nobleman. The author began by lamenting the existing system of values, because "the heredity of virtuous actions is valued less than ... the possession of wealth." He then considered the nobility's loss of positions: the nobility having neglected its education, very few nobles were qualified to serve as councillors, and consequently moneyed families had taken their place. In recent years, efforts had been made to correct these conditions, but they had been ineffectual. "Now at last you, sire [Richelieu], have given us hope that hereafter ambition and riches will not be prized over courage and virtue."[75] It was by now a familiar lament. And perhaps we can even detect a tone of futility in the recognition that determined efforts, even when supported by the Estates General and the king, had not succeeded in reinstating the nobility in its public and governmental role.

IV

The failure of the attempt to reassert the nobility's importance in the government of France is not surprising. For one thing, the effort lacked direction and consistency. It failed to concentrate on a few key positions of major importance, and instead repeatedly shifted and confused the objectives, betraying not only a lack of coordination, but also an unawareness of the difference between positions that were the real pivots of political power and ones that were being emptied of their practical significance. In short, the nobility showed a vitiating uncertainty about whether it was primarily interested in actual service or in mere sinecures, whether it sought a recognized function or merely pensions and perquisites.

The effort was also handicapped by stereotyped ideas of proper noble activity. How much, for instance, was the emphasis on the Maison du Roi, the military commands, and the position of bailli due to the assumption that the nobility's primary function was military? And how were the nobility's efforts to gain judicial posts to be reconciled with the persistent notion that the practice of law was demeaning? Despite all the efforts we have examined, these basic conflicts were never wholly resolved.

Even more significant perhaps was the nobility's anomalous position with respect to the question of whether offices should be distributed on the basis of personal merit or sold for money.

Either way the nobility would suffer. To be sure, by proper education the nobles might have become able to compete on the basis of merit. But the educational programs were not fulfilled. Perhaps the idea was never really feasible anyway without a complete social upheaval, for implicit in all arguments for merit and education was the idea of an elite as opposed to a hereditary aristocracy. On the other hand, the possibility (suggested at least once) that the nobility might live with the practice of venality, using its own wealth as a means of recovering political importance, was out of the question in view of its economic debility. What actually developed, therefore, was a three-way tug of war, a struggle among three opposing principles of advancement: venality, merit, and class status. To argue for preferment strictly on the basis of noble birth was a lost cause, as the practice of venality ultimately became. But the struggle continued, in one form or another, until the Revolution and beyond.

The nobility of the old regime was not a true "service" nobility. Neither in military service nor in public service did it succeed in regaining dominance; neither of these was its specifically recognized *class* function. When attempts to rectify the situation met with little success, the rationalization of noble privilege was made more difficult, and the self-esteem of nobles was weakened. Class pride did not disappear, of course, but the malaise of aristocrats was intensified by the awareness that (in the words of our pamphleteer of 1567) "it would not be possible to ruin" the nobility "more easily than by rendering it useless, which is what will happen if it is not employed."

CHAPTER 4

The Rule of Dérogeance

The Thracians, the Scyths, the Persians, the Lydians, and almost all other barbarians, hold the citizens who practice trades, and their children, in less repute than the rest, while they esteem as noble those who keep aloof from handicrafts, and especially honor such as are given wholly to war.

—HERODOTUS

Plusieurs de la noblesse vivent de telle façon qu'ilz n'ont de noble rien plus que le tiltre, s'adonnant à toutes traffiques mécaniques, tenant par aferme les heretaiges d'aultruy, achaptant et vendent bled, vins, sel et aultres chouses.

—Cahier from the diocese of Castres

I

Combining to undermine the economic position of the nobility from the end of the Hundred Years' War to the middle of the seventeenth century were the long secular price rise, the division and subdivision of family estates among children generation after generation, and the increasing cost of maintaining an aristocratic pattern of life. The nobles were not, however, entirely helpless victims of circumstance. They could try to mitigate the effects of the trends with improved farming methods and a rational marketing system, increased feudal dues, royal pensions, marriage alliances with wealthy families, investment in trade, or any combination of these. Standing in the way of the last alternative, trade or investment in trade, was the traditional prejudice against nobles' involvement in commerce. It is to this prejudice, as it was expressed between 1560 and 1640, that we turn our attention in the present chapter, for it was at the center of the argument about the nobility's role, its privileges, and its image.

The theory of *dérogeance* provided that a nobleman who participated in activities that were deemed incompatible with nobility would suffer derogation of his privileged status. The idea was hardly new in the sixteenth century; it has probably existed in all societies with hereditary aristocracies.* In the Western tradition we have only to recall the contempt of ancient Greek philosophers and educators for activities that smacked of labor or of sordid gain. The prejudice was retained by the Romans and by the medieval knightly class. In 1295, when Philip the Fair exempted the nobles from paying him a certain aid, he specifically excluded those in trade.[1] In 1435, Charles VII had refused to exempt from taxation nobles who sold their wines in taverns. "It is not the business of nobles," he said, "to be tavern keepers."[2] Early in the sixteenth century, some of the ordinances of Francis I voided the tax exemptions of nobles who meddled in the activities of roturiers.[3] In 1549 the great jurisconsult André Tiraqueau declared emphatically that noble status was impaired by trade.[4] And in 1560, Estienne Pasquier stated that for some time in France it had been considered "derogating" for nobles to engage in commerce.[5]

But while the general idea of dérogeance was very old, it was still unjelled in the early sixteenth century. Paul Viollet, the eminent legal historian, exaggerated when he said that the rule dates only from that period, but it is true that dérogeance was often ignored in the *coutumiers,* or customary law, that the royal ordinances on the subject were of an ad hoc nature, and that several fundamental questions were still unanswered.[6] Only a few years previously, Louis XI had tried to overcome the traditional bias by encouraging nobles to enter commerce—an unsuccessful project, but one that did somewhat muddy the stream.[7]

---

* See, for example, the passage from Herodotus at the head of this chapter.

Then, in 1560, a royal ordinance included a clause clearly forbidding nobles to engage in the traffic of goods on penalty of being subjected to the taille. The prohibition was renewed in 1579.[8] Since the rule of dérogeance as stated in these ordinances remained in effect for more than half a century, it is easy to come away with the impression—if only these high points are considered—that the doctrine was at last firmly established and that our period was totally given to the view that nobles should be excluded from all business and trade. Though partly true, this impression relies too much on the ordinances and fails to recognize the interplay of opposing opinions on a lower level.

II

To start with the opinion most easily overlooked, some persons from 1560 on were anxious, or at least willing, to open up commercial activities to the noble class. There were different degrees of willingness, some wishing the nobles to be allowed to engage in all kinds of trade and others wishing them to be restricted to large-scale commerce; and there were different motives. What the different shades of opinion have in common is opposition to the strict rulings of 1560 and 1579.

One motive for trying to bring nobles into business activities was the desire to avoid the "ruin and destruction of the noble houses."[9] In 1560, some nobles from Touraine asked the king "to allow nobles destroyed by the rigor of the times or by the losses of war to engage in some modest trade or business."[10] This request was turned down, but other nobles, in Marseille, were able to obtain such permission a few years later.[11] The nobles who favored such a solution were relatively few, for reasons that we shall see, but the lure of commercial profits was great. In 1614 at the Estates General the delegates of the Second Estate asked that nobles be allowed to enter "grand commerce"; and in 1627 at the Assembly of Notables a similar request was heard.[12]

All of these requests but the last were rebuffed. "The king

for good and sufficient reasons cannot grant it" was the official answer in 1560; and as we have seen, the ordinances of that year and of 1579 contained firm prohibitions against nobles in commerce. But the opposed idea was not entirely stifled. In fact, it began to be heard not only from impecunious nobles but also, at least as early as the reign of Henry IV, from some influential advisors to the king.

Barthélemy de Laffemas had been a member of Henry's household in Navarre. He was an acute observer and was full of suggestions (which he broadcast in pamphlets) about what the country needed.[13] Having filled a prominent role at the Assembly of Notables in 1596, he was asked two years later to prepare a survey of the country's industry. In 1601, the king endorsed some of Laffemas's proposals and in the following year created for him the new position of Controleur-Général du Commerce. Laffemas does not say much about the nobility in his pamphlets, except for his attempt to persuade the rural nobility to raise silkworms.[14] But in 1597 he did propose that France follow the example of Italy, where the exercise of commerce and industry was not incompatible with nobility.[15] It would be interesting to know just how serious Laffemas was about this, but at least it is clear that he saw certain advantages in breaking away from the old rule.

More influential than Laffemas in many ways was the Duc de Sully, whose role in the reconstruction of France after the religious wars is well known. What of his attitude toward nobles in business? To begin with, he was extremely critical of the nobility as a class. The simple, virile knightly class of earlier times had, in his view, degenerated into a soft and debauched nobility. He wanted to reverse the trend by means of sumptuary taxes and public censors. He felt that for their moral as well as their economic welfare, the nobles should stay on their estates. He did not advocate the participation of nobles in industry, which is not surprising since he took a dim view of most industrial activity. When he thought of commerce, however, and when he thought in terms of the nation's economy, his acceptance of the rule of dérogeance is less than total. He saw foreign trade as a means of accelerating the flow of precious metals into France; and to promote commercial expansion he arranged for the ennoblement of leading merchants in Lyons and elsewhere.[16] It was not merely in individual localities that he opposed the dérogeance tradition: regretting its existence, he encouraged all classes of society to participate in the nation's economic development, and often repeated that France would not surpass her rivals as long as maritime commerce resulted in dérogeance.[17]

The primary motive of these advisors, it seems, was not to aid the nobility but to enable the country to surge ahead economically. Allowing nobles to participate in commerce would not only bring their resources into the general economy but, more importantly, would help to overcome the reluctance of many affluent non-nobles to continue in activities that were presently considered degrading. "The country needs to develop commercially," it might have been argued, "and to stimulate investment and to encourage new enterprises we must get rid of this obsolete notion that such activities are in any way unworthy." Feeble attempts in this direction were made in 1611 and 1615, when chartered trading companies were set up with the provision that "all nobles, officeholders, and other people of quality can freely enter the said society without this in any way derogating from or contravening their nobility, privileges, and qualities."[18] But it was not until 1629, under Richelieu, that a wholesale modification of the rule of dérogeance was achieved.

Before looking at Richelieu, it will be well to notice one other influence working against the old restrictions: the idea that the nobles were idle, or at least were not engaged in the productive occupations of society. Idleness was frequently and widely condemned as the mother of vice. "Man was not born to live with folded arms," said one writer.[19] The bourgeois virtues of hard work and productive activities were praised over and over again. In 1562, the consuls of Saint Médard went so

far as to urge that the king learn a trade.[20] (According to
Thierriat and others, that would be nothing new, for commerce was such a necessary and respectable occupation that
"several kings, princes, and great magnates" had participated
in it.[21]) The theory of dérogeance did not even have to be
mentioned; its condemnation was implicit in a system of values in which nobles were regarded as parasites living off the
labor of the productive classes. Antoyne de Montchrétien, a
pioneer of economic thought, after recognizing that the nobility was "debilitated and languishing" and that its only recognized occupation was that of arms, went on to say that the
three important classes in society were the laborers, the artisans, and the merchants. France should, he said, create a society from which all idle would be excluded.[22] The implications of his argument are inescapable: the non-participation
of the nobles in commerce and trade, whatever might be said
in its favor, meant that they were being carried on the shoul-
ders of the roturiers.

The motives of the remonstrating nobles and those of the
royal economic advisors come together in Richelieu. Unlike
Sully, he refused to participate in the carping criticism of the
nobility. From a family of the lesser nobility himself, he was
aware that all was not well but felt that the nobles could be
of great value to the nation. Perhaps, too, he went further
than Laffemas in stressing the need for commercial expansion
and for increasing the prestige of merchants and traders. Both
for the sake of the nobles and for the economic good of the
country, he felt, the rule of dérogeance had to be relaxed.

It is hard to say just how completely this idea was worked
out in Richelieu's mind in 1624, when he entered the King's
Council. It emerged at the Assembly of Notables of 1626–27,
when the noble delegates requested that they be allowed to
participate in commerce without losing their privileged status;[23] but to what extent it was inspired by the nobles remains
obscure. Neither in Michel de Marillac's important speech before the Assembly nor in the fifteen-point program presented

by Richelieu was the suggestion that nobles be allowed to engage in commerce stated in so many words. Nonetheless, the
idea was certainly in the air. In 1626, for instance, an anonymous work entitled *Advis à messieurs de l'Assemblée des
Notables* concluded its strong appeal to the "notables" for the
reestablishment of France's commerce with this prediction:
"In a short while you will create an immense fleet and cover
the sea with sails; and you will employ a number of the young
nobility who are staying at home and becoming degener-
ate."[24] About all that can be said with any confidence is that
the idea was around, the noble delegates did request that the
restrictions be relaxed, and this may well have been what
Richelieu had in mind from the outset.

A royal declaration in January 1627 stated in a general way
the king's desire to honor commerce so that the merchants
would be content instead of being envious of the privileged
orders.[25] But the new line on dérogeance was not embodied
in a legislative enactment until 1629, when it was written as
part of the Code Michaud: "We decree that all nobles who
become engaged in maritime commerce, either directly or
through proxy, do not derogate from their nobility, without
however being free to do retail business, nor being exempt
from paying import, export, and passage duties on their mer-
chandise."[26] The rule worked two ways, in that some non-
noble merchants (those who ran ships of over 200 tons) would
enjoy noble privileges. Thus the rule of dérogeance in its strict
form was modified; henceforth it would be possible, legally,
for nobles to engage in certain types of commerce without
losing their status.

III

But why had it taken so long to break down the strict rules
of 1560 and 1579? And why was the concession in 1629 so
limited? For some reason the theory of dérogeance had an
extremely strong hold on the French mentality. Obviously
something could be said in its favor. During the same years

that certain pressures had worked to break it down or modify it, there were also arguments put forth in its defense.

One of the most common of these was the appeal to tradition. It had *always* been believed that trade and nobility were incompatible. Had not Plato said as much? And Cicero? Had not all ancient peoples from the Egyptians to the Romans frowned on menial and mercantile activities? And Noah? And Adam? One writer even traced the origins of the prejudice against trade to the angels of heaven.[27]

Similarly, the idea of dérogeance was said to be commonly accepted in many other nations. But here the argument could and sometimes did backfire, for it was plain that a good many modern nations were forgetting about the old restrictions. England, Holland, Portugal, Spain, Italy, Denmark, Poland —all were more or less conceding, at least in practice, that nobles had a place in commerce.[28] However, generally speaking, the defenders of the dérogeance tradition in France either ignored the defections of other nations or shrugged them off as exceptions. While it was true that Italian nobles entered trade, said one, they were regarded by all other nations as having lost their nobility.[29] One author, Thierriat, did recognize, however, that different countries had different standards and that what some peoples thought to be an occupation honorable and noble, others regarded as sordid and dishonorable.[30] This concession allowed the practice in France to be defended, but it implied a cultural relativism that was contrary to the argument of universal acceptance.

But the tenacity of the theory of dérogeance was probably due less to historical precedent or universal acceptance than to the vital self-interest of several groups. For one thing, the idea of having nobles enter business and trade was not relished by the Third Estate. In 1560, when some nobles requested a relaxation of the rule, it was the Third Estate who cried that for nobles to participate in commerce would be "highly indecent." The same attitude was displayed in 1576 and in 1614.[31] To some extent, of course, there was a natural desire to minimize competition, but the explanation usually given was that it would be unfair to allow nobles both exemption from taxation and profits from trade.

The connection between the nobility's exemptions and its abstention from trade was often stated or implied. For example, in 1540, when Francis I forbade nobles to lease property on a share-of-profit basis, he explained that "mechanical and roturier arts" were reserved for those who contributed to the taille.[32] An anonymous writer later explained that nobles were forbidden to enter trade "so that the roturiers who pay the tailles will not suffer."[33] And one could scarcely be more explicit than Loyseau, who explained that roturiers paid more taxes but were compensated in that the nobles did "not participate in the profits of commerce and trade."[34]

The close relationship between dérogeance and privilege becomes clearer when we notice that the prohibitions on trade applied not only to nobles but also to officeholders who were exempt from the taille.[35] A nobleman found guilty of participating in the forbidden activities lost his privileges, but for a long time it was arguable just how far his status was permanently affected.[36] The main point was that one should not enjoy both exemptions and business profits. The rule of dérogeance, in other words, offered a quid pro quo: the Third Estate could tap the country's commercial profits while the nobles enjoyed exemption from taxation. The nobility thus "earned" its privileges not only by making positive contributions to the state but even more by leaving the most lucrative areas of economic life to the roturiers. This view explains fairly adequately, I believe, the reluctance of the Third Estate to admit nobles into commerce.

But how do we explain the fact that most nobles clung to the theory of dérogeance with all their strength? The strict rules of 1560 and 1579 were not, as one might easily assume from the cases cited earlier, forced on a reluctant nobility. It is important to realize this, for once we are aware that the rule of dérogeance was supported generally by king, Third Estate, *and* nobility, we can begin to understand why it was given up so reluctantly and why, even in 1629, the concessions were by no means sweeping.

What the nobles had against commerce, it is sometimes said, was its incompatibility with the conventional picture of ideal noble behavior. Bravery, magnanimity, generosity—these were the virtues especially valued by nobles. Largesse was considered so essential that not a few nobles went heavily into debt in the interest of hospitality and conspicuous display. Unselfishness and willingness to sacrifice—these too were aristocratic virtues. The nobleman was supposed to be ready to give his all in the service of king and country. This was difficult to do, but between 1560 and 1640 the nobility was still making the effort, trying to reestablish its military and public service roles. And how, it was asked, could the required qualities of character, the aristocratic virtues, possibly be reconciled with sordid profit-grubbing? As Oncieu explained it, the nobleman had special responsibilities; it was the "first law of nobility" that he prefer the public interest to his own. Trade would cause him to concentrate on private gain. It was therefore unthinkable that nobles be found in the markets buying things cheap in order to sell them dear, haggling over prices with all kinds of riffraff. The proud arms of nobles were not intended to be dragged through markets, shops, and cabarets.[37]

The true life of the nobleman, according to this view, was spent on his country estates away from the dust and smell of commerce and the corruption of the towns. There the air was purer; there he could keep himself in condition by the hunt; there, where all was tranquil, he could follow the offices of religion more devotedly and thus gain "much contentment." Luxuries were few, but there was an "honest sufficiency" and there was the good company of friends.[38] It is a glowing picture, in the tradition of the nostalgic praise of the rural life that goes all the way back to Virgil or Hesiod. Why did this idealization of life on noble estates become an especially popular theme in the late sixteenth century?

It was a time when the pestilence of war, the buying and selling of offices, the corruption of the court, and the noise of the towns aroused not a little nostalgia for the simple, bucolic life. And those who wanted to see the nobles restored to their sometime preeminence, those who deplored the modern tendencies, looked upon the traditional aristocratic estate life as one of the bulwarks against degeneration. It was all part of "living nobly," or of what was sometimes referred to as the "exemplary life." Such a life was defended as most appropriate for developing the noble virtues, and an effort was made to refute the charge of idleness. If the nobleman were doing what he should, said Oncieu—ministering to the widows and orphans, stopping quarrels between his subjects and his neighbors—if he were ready to answer the call at any time by going to court or by taking up arms in defense of the country, could it really be said that he was idle, that he was useless, that he was doing nothing? He should rather be held in honor.[39]

Thierriat also defended the noble manner of life: "Not without reason did Aristotle say that idleness is necessary for the support of virtue. And Plato, answering those who criticized the life of the philosophers as too restful and idle, said that such idleness was more serious than any other occupation." That was why the nobility of all nations had renounced trade; for the best way to make a person virtuous was to give him time to philosophize, to think of himself, to fill his mind with serious thoughts.[40] This defense might have been received with a snort by those who saw the nobles of their day as uncouth and unlettered, but the theory made some sense. It anticipated Burke's defense of privilege.

Still it would seem that the notion of the noble life could have been revised (as at least some people wished) to allow nobles to take up trade. Why, instead, did the rule of dérogeance seem so important? The answer, I believe, lies primarily in the nobles' desire to counteract the confusion of status by strengthening the distinctions between themselves and roturiers. If nobles plunged into trade, the result, as Du Rivault said, would have been to obliterate "the distinction of estates" and restore confusion.[41] The differentness of the nobility seemed essential to its continued existence, and now that such things as military performance no longer set the nobles apart, the emphasis had to be on special privilege, special dress, and a special manner of living—which included abstinence from trade.

Since there were, as we have seen, arguments both for and against the rule of dérogeance, it is not surprising that an effort would be made to have it both ways. Some, while admitting the general theory, maintained that large-scale commerce was permissible, since it did not involve the petty haggling, the degrading atmosphere, and the meanness of the small retail shops. Even in large-scale trade there was danger of avarice, to be sure, but perhaps this had to be risked in order to save the nobility from economic destruction.[42] This view was taken up by the noble delegates to the Estates General in 1614, and in 1629 this was the compromise adopted.

It needs to be acknowledged that despite the strong support of dérogeance, some few nobles had all along been participating in commerce and industry. It was legally possible, for instance, for nobles to engage in glassmaking, and some did so.[43] Likewise, nobles in Lyons, Marseilles, Bordeaux, and other leading towns had obtained permission, in the form of special royal licenses or charters, to engage in trade[44]—to say nothing of the nobles who got away with investment in business enterprises, often under assumed names, and with secretive trading.[45] Nevertheless, the strong grip of the rule of dérogeance is undeniable. This was true even after 1629, for an attempt in that year to stimulate noble participation in maritime commerce was far from successful. The prejudice was too deeply ingrained to be overcome by a simple act of legislation. In 1700–1701, when a special Council of Trade was convened to analyze the needs of the national economy, one deputy remarked that "merchants and trades are too despised and degraded in France"; and other deputies too "deplored the fact that the average Frenchman was scornful of trade and held merchants in little esteem."[46]

One cannot explain the long-range limitations of France's economic development as stemming primarily from the theory of dérogeance, but it does seem true that France was deprived of the energies and investment potential of her aristocracy to a greater extent than most other countries of Western Europe. And if "entrepreneurial spirit" is important to a nation's economic expansion, then the system of values represented by dérogeance, which was to a considerable extent accepted by the bourgeoisie, must have been a significant handicap.[47]

Finally, what of the effects of the theory of dérogeance on the nobility itself? For one thing, it was handicapped economically. But what was the alternative? "Persons struck with the practice of some states," Montesquieu later remarked, "imagine that in France they ought to make laws to engage the nobility to enter commerce. But these laws would be the means of destroying the nobility without being of any advantage to trade."[48] This observation has a kernel of truth.

The French nobility survived, after 1629, for another century and a half. But it was survival at a price. The nobles of the late sixteenth and early seventeenth centuries recognized their dilemma. What they could not see so well was that the forced choice between usefulness and distinctiveness was the central theme in a long tragedy.

CHAPTER 5

The Relevance of Virtue

Si d'autre part vous mesurez la Noblesse à la seule vertu,
combien, je vous prie, y a il de gens vertueux, ausquels
on ne rend l'honneur qu'ils meritent bien?
—ERNAUD (1584)

La noblesse est une belle qualité, et introduite avec raison; mais d'autant que c'est une qualité dependant d'au-
truy et qui peut tomber en un homme vicieux et de
neant, elle est en estimation au dessoubs de la vertu.
—MONTAIGNE (1588)

Was nobility an inherited quality or was it contingent on
personal virtue? It was an old question. Having been discussed by all the favored classical authorities, who were quoted
and quoted again, and having also been rehashed in Italy
during the preceding two centuries, the issue had become
rather shopworn by the sixteenth century.[1] But although repe-
titious, hackneyed, and to some extent derivative, the continued argument is of interest to us not only because it illus-
trates how contemporaries often saw the issues, but also because it was often related to particular conditions in France.
The large-scale incursions of "new nobles" into the French
aristocracy, for instance, were difficult to reconcile with an
exclusive argument from inherited rank. And the supposed
virtue essential to nobility was in conflict with the misdeeds
and malpractices of many French nobles during the religious
wars. It was in this context that French thinkers were prompted to grapple with the relationship of virtue and birth to nobility. If they borrowed ideas from the past and from other
countries, it was with the desire of applying them to the situation in France, where the old dilemma took on a new relevance.

I

Not surprisingly, perhaps, most contemporaries were willing to side with virtue. But they did so in different ways and to different degrees. A few of them made virtue the sole requirement for noble status—Guillaume de La Perrière, for example, who wrote in 1567 that "there is no true nobility except that which proceeds from virtue and good conduct," and that "whoever by vice makes himself villain should be rejected as a sharp thorn, and whoever by good virtues makes himself smooth and fragrant should be venerated as the rose and regarded as noble, whatever his birth."[2] Similarly, Estienne Pasquier stated that "every man in every estate who attains to virtue and a blameless life is noble, without any exception."[3]

But exclusive reliance on virtue as a criterion for nobility had disturbing implications. The existing class alignment, if virtue were the sole consideration, would have to be drastically revised: not only would irresponsible nobles have to be cast out, but an effort would have to be made to recognize as nobles all who were virtuous. "If you measure nobility by virtue alone," said Louis Ernaud in 1584, "how many virtuous people are there who are not receiving the honor they deserve?"[4]

Therefore, while they stressed the need for virtue, most of the writers who dealt with the subject did not consider it sufficient entitlement for nobility. The distinction is easy to overlook. It amounted to saying that the peasant or the day laborer, however morally impeccable, could not on that account be elevated to the aristocracy, yet that those now recognized as nobles must meet certain minimal standards of "virtue." Tiraqueau, Froydeville, and L'Alouëte all agreed that if the individual ceased to be virtuous he should be deprived of his noble status.[5] Those who base their nobility solely on their ancestry, said Nicolas Pasquier, are like an unfruitful tree that seeks to be admired because of its root or trunk.[6] Even

Noël Du Fail, who saw everything through the eyes of a *noble de race*, allowed that nobles had a responsibility to conduct themselves virtuously.[7]

Nevertheless, most of those who wrote on the subject had no intention of disregarding noble birth. Since this factor loomed so large in the practical determination of status in the sixteenth century, it can scarcely be surprising that many writers continued to include "race" as part—often the central part—of their definition of nobility. What men of the sixteenth century really wanted, it appears, was to have it both ways: to agree that virtue was essential to true nobility while retaining the traditional *noblesse de race* as the noble class. This required a tour de force; the case for noble birth had to be presented in such a way that those who ranked high according to the criterion of birth would be the same as those who ranked high according to the criterion of virtue.

The arguments supporting this proposition were several. First, it was often said that noble status was a reward for the virtuous performance of the original noble ancestor, thus bringing in virtue but not necessarily claiming it for the living descendants. Typical, even in its ambiguity, was the speech of jurisconsult François Grimaudet before the Estates General of 1560, in which he justified the exemptions of nobles by explaining that these exemptions had been conceded to them and their posterity "to repay them for their virtue."[8]

But pointing to the brave and worthy deeds of a distant ancestor did not suffice, particularly as it became more and more popular to criticize nobles who relied solely on the merit of their progenitors. It was necessary somehow to convince people that nobles of the present generation were virtuous. A curious attempt to do this was made by Louis Musset, who explained in 1582 that nobles of race were "preferable to those who by their own virtue and without help from their ancestors" obtained recognition as nobles, because the praiseworthy actions of the latter were probably motivated by presumption or by ambition. Deeds of virtue were much more difficult (hence more apt to be genuine) for the noble of birth, who had to leave behind not only his family, but a large income, comfortable châteaux, gardens, and the pleasures of the chase to perform a military or diplomatic duty.[9] This argument could be of little help to nobles who would not budge from their estates, and in any case one could object that non-nobles too had families and, sometimes, large incomes.

More serious was the argument that superior character tended to be hereditary. This was the expected nobles-are-naturally-superior premise of such old-guard figures as Noël Du Fail, who maintained that roturiers were inferior.[10] But others also gave credence to the heritability of virtue. A Portuguese work, translated into French in 1549, asserted that individual differences were inherent and that both good qualities and defects were transmitted to descendants; this applied to trees, to horses, and to men. Nobility consisted "not merely in custom and manner of life but also in a natural quality of spirit, and in lineage."[11] Though not specifically French, therefore, and not new, the idea was taken up in the latter half of the century by French writers who found that it served their purposes well. L'Alouëte, for instance, considered virtue to pass naturally from father to son.[12] And according to Du Rivault, just as the sun's light shines on the world, the virtue of the original noble ancestor would shine also in his son— "the good are born of the good, and the virtuous of the virtuous." While granting that sons did not always possess the virtues of their fathers, he assured his readers that the lustrous qualities were only temporarily submerged and would shine forth again in the grandson or great-grandson.[13]

This explanation of the bad specimen was at least a partial answer to those who would deprive all non-virtuous nobles of their status. It was taken up again, in 1611, by Nicolas Pasquier, who argued that noble qualities tended to be hereditary, owing to a "secret seed" that was transmitted from generation to generation. Sometimes young noblemen did not exemplify the desired qualities, but, just as with plants of good strain, an occasional inferior individual might well be followed by a generation of better quality than ever. A minor cough, he pointed out, did not destroy the soundness of the body.[14]

If heredity had its proponents, however, there were other people who were more convinced by an argument from environment. Another attempt to bring together aristocratic birth and individual virtue, it attributed the noble's personal qualities to the upbringing and education he received in his family. For instance, La Perrière asserted that it was not race and lineage that made a man noble, but "exercise, education, instruction."[15] Froydeville also emphasized the importance of upbringing, not so much to claim that the home training of nobles was inherently superior, however, as to enjoin nobles to rear their children properly. If parents had punished their misbehaving children, he said, the kingdom would not now be so ravaged and disrupted.[16] Ernaud, while of course recognizing the desirability of personal virtue, defended hereditary status on the ground that only within such a framework could young nobles learn obedience and acquire the skills and qualities required for a military vocation.[17] The all-important influence of noble fathers on their sons, and the consequent excuse for hereditary privileged status, was conceived by Du Rivault almost in Lockean terms: "The blank paper of these new spirits receives his [the father's] own virtues as its first impression."[18]

The necessity of an aristocratic environment for the formation of noble character was carried even further by Florentin de Thierriat, who defended the nobility against the charge of idleness: "The nobility of all nations forbade those within this order to exercise trades because the leading men judged that the way to render a person virtuous was to give him a large amount of leisure in order to philosophize, to reflect on himself, and to fill with great thoughts the reasonable part of the soul."[19]

The most explicit rejection of the notion that virtue was

inborn came from Charles Loyseau. Although nature had provided that plants and animals should inherit the qualities of their kind, he explained, the soul of man came directly from God and thus was not affected by the "generative seed of the body." Quite often worthless children came from good parents. If children sometimes had habits similar to their fathers', this came "not from generation, which contributes nothing to souls, but from education." It was in their education that children were motivated to lives of virtue. Loyseau's concept of education was not narrow; it included careful instruction, the example of the fathers, the felt obligation not to betray the family's honor, and finally the high reputation enjoyed owing to the memory of ancestors.[20]

Not identical with home training and education in the strict sense, although closely related to them and usually stressed by the same authors, was the influence of ancestral tradition in noble families. Family tradition, said Du Rivault, was gradually ingrained in noble children by a thousand little spurs of honor. Deep and abiding values the parvenu could not hope to acquire overnight. Time alone produced perfection, and therefore the ancient nobility should be held in the highest esteem.[21]

II

If these arguments had been convincing, if even one of them had become a common assumption, much of the difficulty over the concept of nobility would have disappeared. The apparent tension and conflict between birth and virtue would have been resolved by showing that the two were identical. That this was not achieved is readily apparent from the polemical nature of nearly all the above arguments. Even within individual writers the tension can be seen; some of them contradict themselves, or at least lack consistency, as they alternately discuss noble birth and personal virtue. Almost all of them tried to work out a compromise formula that would satisfy the demands of both tradition and morality.

Those who seriously defended either extreme were but a few poets and moralists whose concept of nobility was naive or incompletely worked out.

The problem was often posed in the form of a stock question: Of two individuals, one belonging to an eminent family of the old nobility and the other possessing outstanding moral qualities, which should be regarded as superior? One of the most complete treatments was Jean-Baptiste Nenna's treatise on nobility. Although it was first published in Italy in the 1540's, it did not really enter the French current until 1583, when it was translated. Because of its influence on French thinkers and because of its lack of originality, this work is worth considering in some detail.[22]

As it opens, a lady gives her ring to two young men, saying that it should be taken by the nobler of the two and leaving them to determine which one is entitled to the prize. A debate follows in which Possidoine, a noble of blood and wealth, and Fabrice, preeminent in virtue and knowledge, present their respective cases. The judge who renders a verdict at the end of the dispute seems to be the author himself.

Possidoine omits none of the standard arguments in favor of hereditary nobility. Heredity, family environment, the improved character that resulted from living nobly, all are seen as supporting the superiority of race. Did not Jesus Christ Himself enter the world through the noble lineage of David? As for those individuals who had received letters of ennoblement, they are praiseworthy enough, Possidoine supposes, but the letters alone do not make them noble, for riches are necessary if the title is not to be meaningless. And if there is ever a question of priority between two nobles of blood, he whose nobility is more ancient should be preferred. This might not always be easy to determine, as is suggested by a choice anecdote. In Florence there was a dispute about which noble family was the most ancient. It was finally agreed that the honor should go to the Baronses, who were so ugly that they must surely have been the most noble family not only of Florence but of the whole world, having been created when God was still learning how to fashion men.

In rebuttal, Fabrice contends that "true and perfect nobility is not in blood but in the mind." He assails the weaknesses inherent in all arguments for hereditary nobility. Even in basing their own status on that of their ancestors, he points out, the nobles of race have finally to appeal to meritorious actions in order to justify the original bestowal of rank. And if the qualities of true nobility are strictly hereditary, where are the descendants of illustrious Roman nobles, such as Scipio? Further, Fabrice cites numerous examples of sons who did not exhibit the virtue of their fathers. As for the arguments from family background and training, he astutely notes the tacit assumption that nobility manifests itself in actions and behavior — which have to be learned. Fabrice thanks Possidoine for conceding that he is a noble on an inferior level; but this could be true, he says, only if their respective ranks proceeded from the same source and not if his own was from a more praiseworthy and perfect source, namely virtue. In short, says Fabrice, what Possidoine proved with all his arguments was not his own nobility but that of his ancestors, which was not in question. Fabrice's position may be thought of as moderately equalitarian since he denounced hereditary privilege to clear the way for a new, moral aristocracy, a nobility of virtue.

The judge's verdict, pronounced after long deliberation, is in favor of Fabrice. Nobles of birth who are ignorant and violent are denounced in the verdict as "whited sepulchres."

Actually the judge does not regard birth as irrelevant. He divides the nobility into four different categories. First and highest came persons of both noble birth and personal virtue, the so-called *noblesse composée*. Next came those who were preeminent in virtue but not in birth. Then came those who were of aristocratic birth but were lacking in personal qualities. The fourth category, which is rather clumsily fitted into the scheme, was composed of the recipients of letters of en-noblement, the *noblesse civile* or anoblis.²³

Even in this elaborate scale of evaluation the status of the obscure and unrecognized virtuous remained problematical. (Would the virtue of Fabrice, which won the prize, have been sufficient had he not previously been ennobled?) Likewise, the reader is left in doubt about the standing of licentious and irresponsible nobles. They are denounced, they are subordi-nated to the virtuous, but they still seem to be regarded as nobles.* The importance of Nenna's analysis is that it set forth a scale of relative worth that proved sufficiently con-vincing to be repeated, with minor variations, by most French moralists of the late sixteenth century and early seventeenth century.

Typical of its proponents was Eymar de Froydeville. Start-ing with a current problem—the large number of roturiers who had been recently claiming nobility—he directly con-fronted the question of the nature of nobility. He distin-guished three major interpretations, for each of which author-ities could be cited: (1) nobility is nothing more than ancient wealth and good manners; (2) good behavior and good man-ners suffice in themselves to make a man noble; and (3) only those who are descendants of noble parents can be considered noble. Froydeville's book is in the form of a dialogue, but it is not hard to discern his own general position: "race or line-age does not make a man noble or villein."²⁴ He decried noble-men whose actions had been violent and immoral, saying that they prided themselves as nobles and looked down on those who were one hundred thousand times more virtuous than they. They even called the rest of mankind "bastards of

---

* The author does concede that noble status can be lost, but the position of the unvirtuous nobles of race in his structure remains above that of non-nobles. Just below the nobility, although still in a position of esteem, were ranked non-noble but honorable families. Jean-Baptiste Nenna, *Traicté de la noblesse* (Paris, 1583), pp. 205-10.

God," considering only themselves to be legitimate. Such persons had "only the name and title of gentility, their actions giving them the lie at every turn."[25] But while all those who desired to be considered nobles should try to lead a good life, personal virtue would not alone be sufficient basis for nobility. Froydeville was no equalitarian. He placed great importance on education and upbringing and also openly favored the nobleman of ancient race, if he were virtuous, to the upstart of two or three generations. It is probably fair to say that he rejected all three of the alternative positions with which he had started his discussion. The ideal noble for him would be the person of ancient aristocratic family who did not merely preen himself on that fact but gave evidence of virtue by his own behavior.

Another writer who discussed the relationship of nobility and virtue was L'Alouëte. He held that breeding was not sufficient and that those who did not supplement their noble birth with virtuous actions should be deprived of status:

We who know that we were originally created from the earth can send the nobles of this time, who wish to take advantage of the title of nobility and of their splendid ancestry without following the path of virtue, to tuileries and potteries, where they will find their relatives and their marriage alliances.[26]

But it is not clear just how the loss of status would be effected. At one time L'Alouëte seemed to feel that noble sons, even if they were not meeting the requirements themselves, could still profit from the reputation and the luster of their fathers.[27] At another time he described the losing of status as primarily an economic process: nobles were becoming more and more impoverished, "not having the virtue to resist adversity."[28] Still, L'Alouëte may quite properly be considered among those for whom nobility had moral as well as genetic prerequisites.

Louis Ernaud, Seigneur of Chantores, also maintained that virtue was the fundamental and "true" cause of nobility, and its lack a reason for the loss of status.[29] He advised those who sought noble status that virtue was the most likely avenue of advancement, although he recognized that such idealism would run into certain practical difficulties. Nobles whose personal life was a "great reproach," and who, according to Ernaud's premise, should have suffered loss of status, usually escaped punishment; furthermore, virtue was not always rewarded by ennoblement. Although he urged the aspiring roturier not to despair, since others had arrived at noble status by their personal excellence, this merely underlined the fact that recognition of obscure virtue was neither prompt nor inevitable.

David Du Rivault's attitude was somewhat more complex. Recognizing that many roturiers were virtuous and not wishing to despise them, he thought noble status should be granted when it was deserved, thereby strengthening the declining nobility.[30] Yet he noted that these deserving persons only gradually and over a long period of time lost their common "bitterness." This is significant because, despite his apparent concessions to the idea of nobility as virtue, Du Rivault supported the basic assumptions of hereditary status. Having defined noble status as the honorable recognition owed to virtuous men, he is brought to ask why it should be considered hereditary. His answer is that virtue itself tends to pass from father to son, owing to heredity, education, and family tradition.[31] The turbulent war years, which had been a source of grievances for those who demanded that the nobility be held to moral standards, he explained away by saying that the licentiousness was due precisely to the fact that the military had been flooded with non-nobles, who were not motivated by loyalty and honor.[32] Du Rivault's position was another compromise, but one that tended toward the traditional hereditary determination of status.

Just after the turn of the century a comprehensive treatise on nobility by Florentin de Thierriat appeared. Although Thierriat advocated that nobles lacking virtue be expelled from their class, he explicitly rejected the possibility of virtue alone warranting noble status. There were only two kinds of nobility, he claimed, noblesse de race and noblesse civile, and personal virtue was not identical to either of them—"noble race is one thing, virtue another." The status of civil nobility was given by the sovereign prince "to him who could not claim it without his [the sovereign's] permission, even though in virtue he surpassed others of his condition."[33] Although, in his way, he believed virtue was necessary, and although he suggested that social mobility be determined by qualities useful to society,[34] Thierriat was more closely in touch with actual conditions than were those who spoke of a nobility of virtue while failing to spell out its practical relationship to legal status. Explaining that he was "unworthy of such a high revelation," he focused his attention on the facts of life in the France of his day, where he saw only two sources of noble status that had any practical importance—heredity and royal ennoblement.

III

Even those representative thinkers whom we have just examined, by and large moderates trying to set forth a compromise formula, betrayed a certain ambivalence as they tried to retain virtue as at least one of the criteria of status. And yet its inadequacy as a practical yardstick had been unmistakable, and had led several of the most perceptive observers emphatically to deny the identity of virtue and nobility. "They are qualities that have some affinity," said Montaigne, "but there is a great difference between them. There is no need to confuse their names and titles, whereby both of them are wronged. Nobility is a fine quality and introduced with good reason; but as it is a quality dependent on others, and may fall to the share of any vicious or worthless person, in estimation it falls far short of virtue."[35] In 1593, Guillaume d'Oncieu explained that virtue, although the foundation of nobility, was decidedly not sufficient in itself; it had to be recognized by the prince, who could bestow noble status on the virtuous "among others."[36] So, in 1606, Thierriat was merely repeating a commonly held view when he declared noble race and virtue to be distinct.

Despite all the high-sounding phrases about virtue and nobility, there remained certain obstacles that could not be successfully surmounted. For one thing, how was virtue to be defined? It was easy to give a definition, perhaps, but not easy to provide one that would work as a practical yardstick. When the nobleman in Froydeville's dialogues asks how to identify the virtuous, he is told that the virtuous person is one who despises riches, glory, voluptuousness, and life, and who conquers poverty, shame, labor, and death.[37] In 1577, L'Alouëte said that living virtuously meant to "live rightly and well, do one's duty worthily and without reproach, help the poor, help one's neighbor, resist evil, and conquer one's vices and passions."[38] At least one writer, Jean de Caumont, defined the virtue essential to nobility in terms of the religious conflict of the time. For him, all heretics being necessarily liars and villains, there could be no such thing as a Protestant noble.[39] Others saw the virtue necessary for noble status as what we would call public service—virtue "useful to the common life of man."[40] But even within the realm of public service there was ambiguity. "What is this quality of virtue?" asked the moralist Pierre Charron. "Everyone is not in agreement, except that it should be useful to the public."[41] For others the virtue underlying noble status was strictly military,[42] and for still others it was knowledge and wisdom. Military virtue could be defined in such a way as to include a good many qualities of character:

The perfect fighting man is not he who rushes to meet the enemy … but he who is wise and learned in counsel, sober in need, patient in famine, fair in the midst of force, prompt and hardy in action, diligent to follow his objective or the opportunity that appears—in short, he who despises his own comfort and his own life.[43]

With such fuzzy defining of terms, it is not surprising that the so-called nobility of virtue was dismissed in a standard legal work of the early seventeenth century as "purely speculative."[44]

It was perfectly evident that the theoretical nobility of virtue had little if any relationship to the actual noble class. Caumont, after discussing nobility in lofty religious terms, declared impatiently: "I know that there is a perverse nobility, a serpentine nobility, a bastard nobility ... which possesses nothing of the essence of nobility except the origin of the race."[45] Thierriat was not the only person to become impatient with the high abstractions on virtue, deciding to leave this to God in order to discuss the noble class as he saw it.[46]

Some of these problems were in Oncieu's mind when he denied the identity of nobility and virtue:

There is a great difference between nobility and virtue, and it does not follow that whoever is virtuous should be considered a noble. He may be given the title of honorable, honest, master, and other such, which refer to a certain level of virtue. But the quality of noble, if he has no other basis for it, will be taken from him ... because this quality carries precedence, right to bear arms, coats of arms, and other privileges that no one can of himself claim over others, however virtuous he might otherwise be.[47]

Furthermore, simple virtue could not possibly suffice for noble status: "It is a presumption of the law that all are good unless something is proved to the contrary ... and yet it would not follow that all men are nobles."[48] If mere virtue were the sole requisite for nobility, "everything would be confused in the state; there would be as many nobles as men, all men claiming, as they do, to be virtuous."[49]

The importance of this discussion, ranging from idealism to sharp realism, should not be overestimated. To some extent it was conventional, to some extent a game, and yet the question did have many contemporary thinkers highly wrought up and does betray some of opposing notions regarding the character of the noble class. In an effort to rethink the fundamental assumptions of hereditary aristocracy, the inherent dilemma had to be grappled with anew. Since neither extreme position won out, and since the compromise solutions were unstable, the nobility of the Old Regime continued to show signs of confusion in its presuppositions, its justifications, and its objectives. On the one hand, denunciation of noble vices continued to be a popular parlor game. On the other hand, the prestige of aristocratic birth and the trappings of ancient honor continued to be coveted. The nobility of the Old Regime never escaped from this deep-rooted schizophrenia.

The Ambiguity of Noble Status

> Pour le regard de l'usurpation du nom, titres, et armoi-
> ries de noblesse, les loix et ordonnances sont pleines de
> defences portées par icelle. A dire vray, c'est un desordre
> qui diffame infiniement ceste grande province, où vous
> ne sçauriez avoir remarqué un vray gentilhomme de
> race entre dix qui en portent les accoustremens et occu-
> pent les terres nobles.
> —Noël Du Fail (1585)

> Cette confusion de rangs en la noblesse de France, est
> semblable à une nuict qui tient en mesme rang l'honneur
> et la honte, le merite et demerite.
> —Jacques Leschassier (1602)

So far we have seldom bothered about distinctions within the noble class. In discussing the role of the nobility, and in expressing their anti-noble sentiments, contemporary writers seldom saw the need to make fine distinctions. Clearly they were almost always thinking broadly of the old nobility of the sword. In the preceding chapters, I have usually followed the usage of our witnesses in speaking of the nobility without qualification.

I

Nevertheless it is important to recognize that the nobility was not a neat, homogeneous class. Although they did not belabor this point in the discussions we have considered, most writers were fully aware that noble status was confused. The nobility, they complained, had become "bastardized."[1] The "confusion of ranks within the nobility" was deplored, and the king was urged to prevent it.[2] If there had always been some equivocation in drawing the line between nobles and roturiers, never had the situation been as muddled as now. The ambiguity of noble status, deplored again and again, was one of the recurrent themes of the late sixteenth and early seventeenth centuries. To appreciate the incredible complexity of the problem through the eyes of contemporaries, all we have to do is consider some of the characteristic dilemmas that arose when they attempted to give an inclusive description of the noble class.

To begin with, even in the old nobility matters were not always simple. The children of mixed marriages, for example, were increasing in number owing to the desire of many impecunious noble families to establish marriage connections with wealthy roturiers.[3] Generally such children were held to inherit the class status of the father, but there were some provinces that allowed children to inherit noble status through the mother.[4]

Still very much up in the air was the question of illegitimate children. It was easy enough to say, as some authorities did, that they should be excluded rigorously from the nobility, that they should be branded with the ignominious label of a large "B," that they should be called by the surname of the mother.[5] But what if the birth was officially legitimized? Would this remove the stigma of roture? And what of the children and grandchildren of bastards? Did they continue under the handicap of roturier status or revert to the nobility of former generations? That there was still ample room for disagreement on these and other questions is seen by such diverse and contradictory claims as the following: the bastard might be considered a noble if he followed the military profession; he must go by the name of the mother; he could take the name of the father but not his coat of arms; he could take the coat of arms if a special identifying bar were added to it; he was exempt from the taille; he was not exempt from the taille.[6]

But these old problems, though they contributed to the general uncertainty, were not the major cause of status con-

fusion. It was the active upward social mobility in the sixteenth century that more than anything else obscured the distinctions between noble and non-noble. Roturiers, as never
before, were buying up aristocratic estates. Between 1400 and
1550 in the region south of Paris, at least 52 out of 65 lay
seigneuries changed hands once or more, and the same situation obtained, with minor variations, in Poitou, Normandy,
Guienne, and Languedoc.[7] The vast majority of these estates
seem to have been taken over by non-nobles, aptly described
by a modern historian as "la bourgeoisie en marche vers la
noblesse."[8] To be sure, such land transfers would not in themselves have effected a change in personal status, but it was
common knowledge that the wealthy roturier, once he possessed a noble estate, was in an excellent position to assume
an aristocratic manner of living, avoid paying the taille and
the franc-fief once or twice, establish marriage connections
with noble families, and finally become accepted as a full-
fledged nobleman.[9] Such "seepage," coinciding with the large
property transfers, had created, as one contemporary put it,
a great number of Frenchmen "who call themselves nobles
yet are not."[10] These usurpers of noble status, increasingly
numerous, were repeatedly denounced.[11] It was one of the
most vexing problems of the age.

There were others who were not exactly usurpers of noble
status—i.e. they had some legal basis for their claim to nobility
—but who further obscured the boundary separating nobles
from roturiers. Among them were the anoblis. Ennoblements
by means of royal letters patent had been conferred for generations, of course, but they had always been relatively few in
number, and even during the early sixteenth century they did
not constitute a problem of great magnitude. Historian J.-R.
Bloch was able to discover only 183 individual ennoblements
granted between 1514 and 1546—a fairly insignificant number, even if he overlooked that many again.[12] As time went
on, however, ennoblements were sold in greater numbers. In
1573, purely as a financial expedient, 30 letters were put up

for sale in Normandy; and three years later a block of 1,000 letters was placed on sale throughout the kingdom.[18] Between 1550 and 1650, there were at least a thousand ennoblements in Normandy alone.[14] Although it would be fallacious to follow Pierre Lebeurier's suggestion that this proportion obtained for all of France, there can be no doubt that the anoblis had become a group of considerable importance.

On the surface it would seem that the very act of ennoblement would remove an anobli from the region of uncertainty, and it is true enough that there were good reasons for regarding him as a genuine noble. The standard phraseology of the letter seems specific enough: the king ennobled "the said petitioner, his children and posterity, male and female, born and yet to be born," all of whom were to enjoy all the honors and prerogatives of nobles of race.[15] In the few coutumiers where they are mentioned, there is no evidence of efforts to relegate the anoblis to an inferior level.[16] And there were learned authorities who argued that "ennoblement erases all stain and blemish of roturier status."[17] But these statements were contradicted by others. Noël Du Fail, for example, thought that true nobility simply could not be attained by a legal act, and that even the passage of a hundred years could not remove the deep imprint of a status essentially "bastard and illegitimate."[18] Somewhat more moderate writers, such as Le Bret and Thierriat, insisted that children born before the act of ennoblement should continue to be regarded as roturiers.[19] In the early seventeenth century, the jurisconsult Pierre Brillon, looking back at the opinions of the preceding half century, had no difficulty in compiling a sort of *sic et non* on the question.[20]

Often practical distinctions were made between the anoblis and nobles. Anoblis did not always enjoy the same tax exemptions; they had to stand at council meetings where "true noblemen" were seated; they had to sit on the back row at the Estates and were not allowed to vote with the nobles; at times their wives had to wear a distinctive kind of hat.[21] Apparently trivial, such differences had tremendous symbolic importance. They dramatized the ambiguous position of the anoblis: having moved above the large mass of non-nobles in some ways, still they had not achieved a social status equal to that of the old nobility.

Other persons who had a certain legal basis for their claim to nobility, and yet whose position was not beyond controversy, were those supposedly ennobled through holding a particular office. Ever since special royal charters had been extended before and during the Hundred Years' War, the highest officials of certain towns—La Rochelle, Angers, Poitiers, Niort, Bourges, Toulouse, Angoulême, Cognac, Tours, Orleans, Abbeville and others—were considered to have been ennobled. This municipal nobility, or *noblesse de cloche*, was not numerous, but it further complicated the large question of noble status.[22] The same observation can be made about the privileged bourgeoisie in some of the towns, who, without having been specifically ennobled, enjoyed some of the exemptions and tended to refer to themselves as either "nobles" or "nobles hommes."[23]

But of the privileged officeholders, the most important in the long run were those who claimed noble status on the basis of high administrative and judicial office: the so-called *noblesse de robe*. It would be wrong to think of this group as having been coherent or self-conscious in the late sixteenth century. Even the least controversial of the claimants—the presidents and councillors of the Parlements—were regarded with hostility and suspicion. The king heard complaints that they pretended to be nobles.[24] There was even more resistance with respect to the lower courts.[25] Although the term noblesse de robe was used occasionally around the turn of the century, there was no unanimity on what it meant.[26]

The connection between office and noble status was not simple at all. What of the posts that (as noted in Chapter 3) were supposedly reserved for nobles? If a roturier held one of these positions, as many did, did he become a noble? There were other positions and activities that, although not reserved for nobles, were described as "honorable," or compatible with noble status. One motive for so designating these offices was to open up areas of gainful employment for the old nobility. But another result was inevitable: those already in the honorable occupations began to be surrounded by an aura of nobility.

One such honorable profession, at least according to many authorities, was law. In Dauphiny, lawyers who exercised their offices at the Parlement of Grenoble were for a time considered nobles. There were long fights in the courts on the matter, and finally in 1602 the privileges were declared nonhereditary. But lawyers still enjoyed exemption from the taille, and the question of whether they could properly be considered nobles continued to be raised, as in 1610, 1661, 1668, and 1696.[27] In Brittany, it was held that judges and lawyers "do not derogate from noble status," which I take to mean that nobles could hold these positions without suffering loss of status. In 1544, 1545, and again in 1562, individual lawsuits established that lawyers there would enjoy the same exemptions as nobles. Finally, in 1613, on the basis of these various judgments, it was declared that in Brittany "lawyers are noble"—a characteristically ambiguous clause.[28]

To be sure, some of the confusion was semantic. In a lawsuit in 1610, one Jean Meunier, a former lawyer then living at Chartres, was enjoined by the royal *procureur* from calling himself a noble.[29] When Meunier appealed, the Cour des Aides at Paris reversed the lower ruling, holding that he could call himself a noble "by virtue of his being a lawyer." That the title did not signify a great deal in this instance, however, is shown by the fact that Meunier was not given exemption from the taille or any of the other privileges "that the nobles and gentlemen of France enjoy." When a similar question came up later in the century, the counsel defending the right of lawyers to be called nobles explained that they did not mean to claim "the exemptions of veritable nobility" but merely the title.[30]

But even if it had been agreed precisely which offices were

ennobling—and it had not—other questions remained, particularly concerning the heritability of the acquired status. For example, if a father held a position that was recognized as ennobling, and his son did not take over that same position, was the son noble? If the son did take over the position, did the grandson have to do the same, or did there come a point at which the status became personal rather than merely an attribute of the office? What was the status of other children, brothers and sisters, who were unable to occupy the office? Were there offices that did not confer noble status on the first generation, but did so on the second or third generation if retained in the same family? In the late sixteenth century the answers to such questions were uncertain, contradictory, or changing. Yet until acceptable answers were forthcoming, although many might claim to be nobles by virtue of office, the real meaning of their status was elusive.

For purposes of analysis we have considered separately the usurpers, the anoblis, and the officeholders. These were not mutually exclusive groups, however; letters of ennoblement were often obtained by usurpers and officeholders, and the separate groups merged to some extent through marriage. In the idiom of the day they were all lumped together, usually pejoratively, as "new nobles," a broad term that, for us, is sufficient for most purposes but that should not be allowed to obscure the underlying complexities. "We have in France," said one observer, "a new edition of noblemen—of all calibers."[31]

It is hard to say just how numerous the new nobles were, but some estimates are available. According to an estimate in 1660, only about one-twentieth of the nobility could trace their ancestry back to the feudal families of the Middle Ages.[32] There were possibly fewer new nobles a century earlier, but Noël Du Fail, writing around the middle of the sixteenth century, said "There is only one true noble of race out of ten who carry the accoutrements and occupy noble lands."[33] In 1578, Pierre d'Origny estimated that of five hundred noble families only ten would be "entières," that is, undiluted by roturier blood.[34] These statements must be regarded as impressions only in this pre-statistical age (it is hard enough to get satisfactory figures even on specific legal acts such as ennoblements), but there can be no question that the new nobles were numerous. "There is scarcely a lawyer's son, treasurer, merchant, collector, or other person of modest condition," said the Second Estate in 1588, "who does not falsely claim the name and title of noble."[35]

Denunciation and ridicule were poured on their impudent heads. They received such appellations as villains, usurers, thieves, schoolmasters, shopkeepers, profiteers, and vermin.[36] Their acts of chivalry, it was said, had been performed in shops, in mills, and on farms.[37] To make up for their lack of titles they simply chose some "roche ou pré," and then "voilà Monsieur de la Roche ou du Prèd."[38] They were said to be "for the most part children of our collectors, those who lease our land, or the sons of blacksmiths."[39] Only occasionally was this mixture of contempt and anxiety challenged by a voice protesting that, despite their origin, they were nobles.[40]

II

What was needed, as many contemporaries saw it, was a strict drawing of class boundaries. Just as captains avoid leading their troops into battle at night, because then there is neither honor nor shame, said Jacques Leschassier, so the sovereign should prevent "confusion of orders and ranks among his subjects."[41] The same mood can be detected in L'Hospital's demand that the "bornes," or boundaries, of society be respected; and in the decision of the Brittany Estates to set up a railing (which we might regard as symbolic) between the seats of the delegates of the nobility and those of the Third Estate.[42] To restore "good order," to "separate and discern the nobles," to establish "some difference between the noble and the roturier"—such phrases indicated a widespread desire.[43]

The practical question of how this clarification might be achieved was answered in different ways. Some felt that the problem was largely due to the ease with which many of the traditional marks of nobility could be assumed by non-nobles: the privileges of nobility, ranging from tax exemptions to special treatment in the courts, were not always conspicuous, or useful as insignia.[44] Exemption from the taille was shared by many privileged roturiers. The traditional noble military service, as we have seen, was widely evaded by nobles and to some extent taken over by roturiers. Even the franc-fief, a tax supposedly paid by all non-noble fief-holders, was not wholly satisfactory as a sign of status.

It is against this background—a high rate of infiltration across class boundaries, the old nobility's strong desire to sharpen the boundaries, and the recognition that the traditional marks of status were inadequate for this purpose—that we can begin to understand the intense, obsessive concern with honorific privileges. These included the rights of nobles to precedence in processions, in seating, and even in arrangement of tombs, to special deference in polite salutation, and to special types of clothing and accessories. These indicators of status were not new, but as the interclass boundaries became increasingly blurred they acquired heightened importance. It is significant that vestimentary distinctions were the subject of edicts or ordinances 13 times between 1540 and 1615.[45] To be sure, other reasons were sometimes given for this legislation: to protect public morals, to relieve the French from "Italianate" standards of luxury, to cut off the flow of wealth from the country.[46] But the overriding purpose of it, to judge from the frequency with which it was stated, was to bring into sharp relief the differences between classes. The honorific distinctions should be strengthened, said the cahiers, "to differentiate the nobles from the Third Estate," "to separate and discern the nobles from the roturier and the plebeian"; by means of the honorific distinctions, "the difference between nobles and roturiers" could be seen, and one could determine the status "of all persons."[47] Usually it is only with reference to the heightened concern about class differentiation that the anxiety about feathers and furs makes any sense at all.

The trouble with the vestimentary laws, as might be inferred from the necessity of frequently reaffirming them, was that they were practically impossible to enforce. In one of Noël Du Fail's dialogues a character observed that no one any longer paid any heed to differences of dress—even the peasants covered themselves with silk. "Yes," another character replied, "the French are like the Athenians, exceptionally good at making laws but very lax in observing them."[48] Thus Ronsard's poem addressed to the king was more wishful thinking than anything else:

> Le velours, trop commun en France
> Sous toi reprend son vieil honneur,
> Tellement que la remonstrance
> Nous a fait voir la différence
> Du valet et de son seigneur.[49]

Just after the turn of the century, Thierriat observed, "The ban is everywhere so disregarded that if the nobleman were to cease wearing his sword, there would be nothing in his clothing to differentiate him from a shop clerk."[50] In 1614, an anonymous author complained to the king that the aristocratic silk and velvet were worn by "a great number who have neither title of nobility nor office of magistrate."[51] But it did little good, or was at best a halfway measure, to insist that only nobles could wear silk and velvet when there were groups whose legal standing was still uncertain—the bastards, the anoblis, the officiers, and others. The question of their exact status was essentially a legal one. Obligations in the way of taxation, franc-fief, and military service could not be determined unless a person's legal status were known. The same was often true of inheritance, for the rules of intestate succession among nobles, however they might vary from one province to another, differed from the rules governing intestate succession among roturiers. Cases involving taxation and inheritance clogged the dockets all during the period of this study. Gradually, as many individual cases were judged and effective precedents were established, some of the confusion began to be partially dispelled.[52]

Coming under noble succession might seem close to being recognized as a nobleman; but there was a difference. For example, at first one could not legally claim exemption from the taille, let alone noble status, merely because he came under noble succession. But here, too, contrary precedents were gradually established. In 1575, the Parlement of Paris held that one could claim nobility if his father and grandfather had been nobles "living in the noble style." In 1593, this was applied specifically to the children of the councillors of Parlement: they were to be regarded as nobles if the position had been in the family for three generations. It was not clear whether the grandson was a nobleman of blood or of robe.[53] But it is clear that certain officeholders, specifically those in Parlement, were receiving legal support for their claims to noble status.

The position of the anoblis was also being clarified through court decisions. In 1577, it was ruled that ennoblement included the children born before the act of ennoblement (a question on which there remained some difference of opinion); and in 1595 it was declared that the heirs of anoblis, even collateral heirs, would come under the rules of noble succession.[54]

Even the insecure status of bastards was the subject of legal clarification, although it was probably not to their liking. In a key lawsuit of 1598, the plaintiff claimed noble status on the grounds that his father was a nobleman and that his own birth had been legitimized. He was told, however, that nobility was a matter of blood, that blood could not be changed even by royal fiat, and that therefore a legitimized son could not be considered noble. Even if he obtained a certificate of ennoblement, he would be a mere anobli and not a true noble of race. The principle was stated in 1598, in 1600, and again in 1602: "the bastards of nobles and their children will no longer enjoy noble status.... The exclusion will extend to legitimized bastards."[55]

III

Although these decisions helped make noble status somewhat less ambiguous than in the past, legal cases—ad hoc by nature—did not adequately cover the meaning of noble status and its variations. It is not surprising that a general definition of noble status was wanted, and that large syntheses, another manifestation of the reaction against the confusion of status, began to proliferate.

In 1577, there appeared a treatise on nobility by François de L'Alouëte, a lawyer and officier, bailli of Vertus, who in the next few years advanced to the position of Conseiller du Roi. Recognizing that the nobility was fallen and despised, L'Alouëte went further than most in trying to analyze the trouble, determine its cause, and recommend remedies.[56] The noble class, as he saw it, could be divided into two groups: those who were born nobles and those who were made nobles. Among those born nobles were nobles of race, nobles of medium antiquity, and a *troisième espèce de nativité*, consisting of those whose fathers and grandfathers had been regarded as nobles. As for the second group, those who were made nobles, L'Alouëte allowed three avenues to noble status: military exploits, letters of ennoblement, and certain offices.

The real problem with regard to the officeholders, as we have seen, was simply which offices ennobled and which did not. L'Alouëte listed certain ones that were, in theory, reserved for nobles and that would therefore ennoble any roturier who held them. These included the positions of Peer of France, Constable, Marshal, Provincial Governor, Gentilhomme de la Chambre, "and the like." The lack of precision in the final phrase is noteworthy. He then considered some other officeholders: the Chancellor, the Maître des Requestes, the presidents and councillors of the Parlements, ambassadors of *robe longue,* secretaries of state, secretaries of finance, secretaries of the chanceries, and "in general all similar officeholders of the pen who are now drawn from the body of roturiers and the Third Estate." It was these who were pressing for recognition as nobles, and some of them—notably the presidents and councillors of the Parlements—with considerable success. For L'Alouëte, however, they were all "true roturiers and should not be considered as being on the level of nobles," for they did not "follow the manner of living or the occupation that must be the vocation of nobles."

Yet L'Alouëte's position was not as unyielding as it first appears. He admitted that these "officeholders of the pen" had the privileges and rights of nobility because they were occupying places that traditionally belonged to the nobles. He admitted that their descendants could inherit their positions. In fact, they were so close to noble status that if their children decided to follow the "vocation of nobility," they would at that very instant be accepted on the level of nobles and their descendants would be "true nobles." What did L'Alouëte mean by vocation of nobility? Would a brief term of military service suffice? Would it be enough to be simply inscribed on the rolls of the ban et arrière-ban? L'Alouëte does not say. In any case, it is clear that for him these officeholders occupied an intermediate position; almost but not quite nobles, they enjoyed what later authorities called semi-nobility. The new nobles should not have been too discouraged by this schema. The simple device of incorporating the troisième espèce de nativité as full-fledged "born nobles" meant, in effect, that the anoblis and the officeholders who were made nobles could look forward to the time three generations hence when their grandchildren would be elevated to the nobility of race.

L'Alouëte was aware, of course, that it would do little good merely to arrange neat compartments on paper. He recommended four specific measures. First, all fiefs should remain in noble hands. A utopian scheme, this would have removed all uncertainty about roturier fief-holders, since there would be none. Second, nobles were not to marry roturiers. If they did so, or if the noble parents found it necessary to marry their children into wealthy roturier families, they no longer deserved to be nobles. Third, each nobleman should be able to trace his genealogical lineage and to provide the necessary supporting evidence. Genealogical records were important to L'Alouëte's whole scheme, in which much depended on a strict counting of generations. Finally, nobles should be well acquainted with the vestimentary and other distinctions that set nobles apart from non-nobles. Presumably this would make it easier for the young nobleman to avoid falling in love with a pretty roturière.

L'Alouëte's work, which first appeared in 1577, does not rest primarily on legal precedents. By the turn of the century, however, litigation had produced partial answers to some questions. Then appeared the important edict of March 1600, which firmly stated that bastards could not "assume the title and quality of nobility without obtaining our letters of ennoblement."[57] The same ordinance noted that during the recent troubles many had borne arms, or claimed to have done so, and on these grounds usurped nobility. Accordingly, they were forbidden to "infiltrate into the body of nobility" if they were "not born of a grandfather and father who had followed the profession of arms or had served the public in certain honorable offices, those which, according to the laws and customs of the kingdom, can provide the beginning of noble status for posterity."[58] Here was an authoritative recognition that "certain offices"—unfortunately they were not clearly specified—could bring the holders noble status in three generations.

Soon after this, Cardin Le Bret, who had acquired a reputation for legal acumen at the Cour des Aides and at the Parlement of Paris, explained that offices conferred noble status in either one of two ways. There were some offices that conferred "a full and complete nobility," such as those of Chancellor, Garde des Sceaux, members of the King's Council, secretaries of state, and "all the leading offices of the military, of justice, and of the royal household." Other offices provided not immediate noble status but rather a means of reaching that level: if the father and grandfather held a given office until their death, and enjoyed exemption from the taille and other subsidies, the third generation could claim to be "fully noble." Such offices of semi-nobility were the Councillors on the Sovereign Courts, Treasurers-General of France, secretaries of the king and the royal household, captains and lieutenants of military companies, "and several others."[59]

All of this was an improvement, but ambiguity had not been wholly removed. There was, for instance, a puzzling reference in the first category to "conseillers d'Etat servans actuellement." If one enjoyed noble status only while actually serving in the position, the phrase "full and complete nobility" was seriously qualified. Or was the phrase intended merely to prevent a retroactive application? In the second category there is the characteristically dangling phrase, "and several others," which scarcely met the need for precision.

There were still some persons who refused to accept change. For instance, in 1600, François Ragueau described the nobility of France as consisting only of nobles of race and those "ennobled by letters of the king, duly verified," making no place whatsoever for nobles of robe and of office.[60] But by the early years of the seventeenth century, the weight of authority, including royal edicts and the opinions of the most respected jurists, supported the more flexible interpretation that allowed a modified noble status to certain officeholders. It was a waste of time to discuss all kinds of nobility of virtue, said Jean Bacquet, for in France there were only nobles of race and anoblis. Ennoblements could be either by means of letters or through holding certain offices, and in the latter case three generations had to pass before the transition to noble status was complete.[61] Bacquet was an avocat of the king at the Chambre des Trésors. His analysis reflects the more or less accepted answer—and the impatient mood—at the end of the sixteenth century.

In 1606, there appeared the most monumental treatise on nobility since Tiraqueau's work of 1549. The author, Florentin de Thierriat, was identified on the title page as "Escuyer Seigneur de Lochepierre, Longuet, Saint Navoir, Raon au Boys &c," and he seems to have regarded himself as a noble of race.[62] Many of the ideas were distinctly unoriginal, having been drawn from earlier works and from stock platitudes, but it would be unfair to dismiss the whole work for this reason. Although he had profited from earlier works, especially Tiraqueau's treatise in Latin, Thierriat wished his work to be applicable to actual conditions in France in his time.[63]

He dealt with the familiar problems of deciding what offices were ennobling, how new nobles stood in relation to the old, and what credentials could point up these distinctions and exclude usurpers. He did not elaborate on the position of the officeholders very much, except to explain his opinion that there were certain offices exempted from the taille which were not on that account regarded as ennobling.[64] He did, however, deal at some length with the question of ennoblement, insisting on a strict, legalistic interpretation: since there were only two kinds of nobility, nobility of race and civil nobility, neither of which was identical to personal qualities, it could not be said that anyone was ennobled by virtue or merit.[65] Even so, he held liberal views on the relative flexibility of the class structure. He considered it unreasonable that a gifted person should spend his lifetime in a lowly or menial position. Kings, he explained, should look over their subjects in a fatherly manner, favor those who were virtuous, and relegate to lowly condition those who were "vile and mechanical." Kings thus had the right "to diminish one of the estates of the country in order to augment another" whenever they considered it "useful and appropriate."[66] Royal supremacy and legal clarity came first, but from a broad perspective Thierriat came close to advocating an aristocracy of merit.

The knotty problem, once the different kinds of nobility were listed, was how these groups were related. It is one of the major themes of Thierriat's work that "there are degrees among the noblemen and preference for some over others."[67] The anoblis, whatever their claims, were simply not on a par with the old nobility, although they were preferred to the roturiers.[68] This was to recognize a hierarchy within the nobility, at least in broad terms as between the old nobility and the anoblis.

The crux of the whole matter was how one went about proving his noble status. The burden of proof, Thierriat said, rested on the claimant, who should show that his father and grandfather lived nobly, followed the profession of arms, held noble offices or dignities, associated socially with nobles, wore the accoutrements of nobility, enjoyed exemption from the taille, and were generally reputed to be nobles. Reliable evidence would be required: baptismal records, marriage contracts, treasury registers, muster rolls, and the like. Witnesses, at least four in number and either nobles or officeholders, could testify to whether the parents and grandparents lived in the noble manner. On strictly genealogical questions, actual inscriptions, records, and documents of title were to be insisted upon.[69]

Thierriat repeated the old chestnut about the natural superiority of the nobility of race, but on the whole was in fairly close touch with the conditions of his day. His views on the status of bastards, for instance, were based on his personal observation that in France many of them were enjoying noble status "without contradiction."[70] To the question whether impoverished nobles had the same right as other nobles of refusing to go before a roturier judge, requiring the judge to come to them instead, Thierriat replied, perhaps with a tired smile, let the judge go to them, for they are having enough trouble already.[71] Whatever he may have derived from earlier writers, he was clearly aware of the actual conditions surrounding him.

About the same time—the first decade of the seventeenth century—studies on such subjects as seigneurial justice, rents, office, and orders were being written by the jurisconsult Charles Loyseau.[72] He is far better known than the obscure lawyers and jurists who provided grist for his mill. He grappled with the same problems, however, and he shared the common desire to find some order and reason in the class structure. Now that some of the debris had been cleared away by litigation, precedent, and royal ordinance, a powerful, synthesizing mind such as Loyseau's could hope to discern some order and principle behind the confusion we have been considering.

On the question of bastards, he began by mentioning that almost all authorities considered them exempt from the taille, but that this had been negated by the edict of 1600, which held that they must be officially ennobled in order to enjoy noble status. He then added his own opinion: the ruling of 1600 was too rigorous, contrary to custom, and unfair. It would be more equitable if bastard children were simply regarded as being one step lower on the social scale than legitimate children: the bastards of kings would be princes, those of princes would be seigneurs, those of seigneurs would be gentilshommes, and those of gentilshommes would be roturiers. Even this was mellowed by allowing that the subsequent marriage of the father and mother would have the effect of raising bastards to complete equality with the other children.[73]

Loyseau was clearly aware of the usurpation of noble status, but he did not examine it at great length, perhaps because it was by definition illegal and therefore a problem of enforcement more than anything else. But he did object to the practice of allowing noble status to be acquired by merely showing that one's father and grandfather had been thought to be nobles. Prescription thus had the effect of legalizing usurpation; and as long as this was possible, prohibitions would be of little avail. Clear evidence of roturier ancestry, even if it had escaped detection for three generations, should relegate a person to roturier status. (This referred to those who were claiming nobility of race by prescription and not, as we shall see, to anoblis or officeholders.) Moreover, Loyseau added, the testimony of two or three friends should not be accepted as proof of nobility in lieu of adequate documentary evidence.[74] By focusing on prescription and evidence, Loyseau was striking at the heart of the problem of usurpation.

The practice of ennoblement—granting certificates of nobility to certain roturiers, usually in return for a financial payment—interested Loyseau. He provided a high-sounding rationale for the procedure. The king could confer noble status upon someone of exceptional virtue to reward him and to stimulate others to be equally virtuous. The fee that the roturier paid was to compensate the king for the future loss of taxes and the common people for their increased tax load.[75] Opposing those who thought that "true nobility begins only with the third generation," he maintained that the new status extended not only to children born after the official act of ennoblement but also to those born before.[76] He also asserted that ennoblement purged the blood of all stain of roture, but he recognized that anoblis actually were not esteemed as highly as nobles of race "in the opinion of men."[77] Though he was relatively broad-minded in his attitude toward the anoblis, Loyseau did not close his eyes to social reality.

It was when he came to the question of offices that Loyseau was at his best. His large work *Cinq livres des droits des offices* looked at that phenomenon from every conceivable angle. Inevitably he said something about the connection between offices and noble status; characteristically, he made some careful distinctions: certain officeholders were merely privileged, such as the officiers in the Chambre des Comptes, and should be strictly distinguished from nobles; some higher offices allowed one to assume the title "noble homme."[78] This unfortunate expression, which we noticed earlier, was described by Loyseau as meaning not of the "true nobility" but of "an honorary, improper, and imperfect nobility, which is contemptuously called *noblesse de ville* and which in reality is the bourgeoisie." Loyseau observed that despite the ordinances forbidding non-nobles to wear noble clothing, the wives of these privileged officers did so anyway—clear evidence for him of the "equivocation" or ambiguity of the word "noble."[79]

Another category of officeholders was made up of those whose positions entitled them to "personal" nobility, which in this context meant that the acquired status was not transmitted to the children. Included in this category were the Secretaries of the King, the councillors of Parlement, and the councillors of the other sovereign courts.[80] It is important to note that there were still differences of opinion about the heritability of acquired status. Loyseau himself said that it became hereditary if the office remained in the same family for three generations.[81]

Finally, at the top of the officers were those who received a "true" and hereditary nobility: the officiers of the Crown, the chief officers of the royal household, members of the royal Council of State, heads of sovereign courts, provincial governors and lieutenants, governors of certain chartered towns, and captains and lieutenants in the ordnance companies. These persons were not only considered nobles but were included in what Loyseau called the "high nobility."[82] Since this high nobility supposedly had advantages of precedence over the "simple" nobility, he was saying in effect that certain parvenus were esteemed more highly than, for example, the impoverished families of the rural nobility, which he would place in the "old" but "simple" category. Here, as in other passages, Loyseau's essential flexibility comes through. He was probably closer to recognizing actual social practice than those who were more rigid; but he knew that there was a difference between theoretical status and "the opinions of men," and he knew that his system was not accepted by everyone.[83]

Loyseau's treatise on *ordres* appeared in 1613. The following year another attempted synthesis was set forth in an anonymous pamphlet written by a spokesman for the nobility at the Estates General of 1614.[84] It is the last of the large attempts at synthesis we will consider.

The problem, according to the author, was basically that the old nobility had lost its special functions in the state to new elements of society and that in the process the distinguishing marks of nobility had become meaningless. There were no longer "any marks of difference between them and us, neither in positions, grades, and qualities nor in arms and clothing, unless in the fact that in all these things they have more than we."[85] The old nobility, he explained, was greatly disturbed to see that the title of nobility, acquired with so much esteem and glory, was being sold "for a small amount of money to all kinds of people, even to those most lowly and unworthy.[86] Furthermore, fifteen or twenty thousand persons were "living as nobles, without having any pretext except the fact that they were officiers of finance or justice, or the children of such officiers."[87]

It was this last group of parvenus, the officeholders, that most aroused the author's anger. They acknowledged membership in the Third Estate, he charged, only in order to gain a seat in the Estates, but outside of it they called themselves nobles. If they were nobles as they claimed, they should have left others to represent the Third Estate—genuine merchants, those who really contributed to the taille. They did not do so for fear that such representatives would launch a legislative attack on them.[88]

More interesting than the author's analysis and his caustic tone was his proposed remedy. He would start by revoking all purchased ennoblements of the past forty years. Those whose fathers "had no other title except merchants, laborers, or artisans would again be subjected to the taille"—a reasonable policy, since "they did not pay for their noble status one half of what they would have paid in taxes since their ennoblement."[89] As severe as this proposal seems, the author did not advocate the abolishment of all past ennoblements, but would allow those that had been based on service.

To clarify relationships within the nobility, he wished to make distinctions between the status of gentilhomme and that of noble, and among the positions, grades, estates, and offices that each of them might attain. The distinction between gentilhomme and noble had some basis in usage, and it had been mentioned by Loyseau, but never before had the distinction been made so explicit.

The "gentilshommes" would be those whose noble status could be traced back at least two hundred years, or who had acquired it more recently by arms or by performing some act of valor for the king. (It was assumed that no one could improve his status in this way without having risked his life, and it was not the common soldier who would be so rewarded but the captain of the regiment.) The "nobles," on the other hand, were those whose status was clearly acquired, simple soldiers who had performed acts of valor, for instance, or those who had been ennobled by the king for some non-military service. Also included among the "nobles" were lawyers whose probity and knowledge had won them appointments as councillors in the Parlements and Cours des Aides, as avocats and procureurs of the same courts, or as lieutenants-general of the "sièges présidiaux." Money would not corrupt this new classification, for both ennoblements and offices were to be strictly non-venal.[90]

There were to be careful distinctions in the realm of precedence and symbolic appurtenances, but more important was the careful listing of positions for which the two groups were respectively eligible. Restricted to gentilshommes were the offices, mostly military, of captain of gendarmes, member of companies of gendarmes, captain of light cavalry (*chevaux legers*), maistre de camp in the regiments, captain in the regiments, or gentilhomme in the Chambre du Roi. On a slightly lower level were the positions for which nobles too were eligible, including lieutenant in the chevaux legers, archer in the ordnance companies, and ordinary soldier.[91] Certain non-military offices were also to be reserved for gentilshommes: the presidents of Parlement, of the Cour des Aides, and of the Chambre des Comptes are named. It is not quite clear whether they were to be gentilshommes as a prerequisite for holding the position or whether the status might come as a result of the appointment. Other officials—the councillors, avocats, and procureurs of the above courts—were likewise to be gentilshommes or, as the author added, "at least nobles."[92] This is a bit puzzling especially when considered alongside the earlier statement that councillors, avocats, and procureurs were ranked as nobles.

Though the proposed distinctions would clarify relationships and sharpen boundaries, the author recognized that there would be vertical mobility between roturiers and nobles and between nobles and gentilshommes. Some exceptions would be made "in order not to exclude outstanding men from the offices that they are able to merit."[93] However, the concession was not generous: a roturier who coveted a councillorship, for instance, would be considered eligible only if he had served for ten years as an avocat with great distinction.

So that each individual's place in the new scheme would be clear, there needed to be some kind of official listing of ranks.* This would be accomplished by having the procureur-general prepare a roll for each bailliage. Titled gentilshommes would be listed first, followed by other gentilshommes, and finally by the "nobles." The roster would be posted in a public place

---

* This author's proposal for an official roster of the nobility was not the only one in our period. Nicolas de Montand's suggestion of such a roster was only one example among several in the late sixteenth century. Montand, *Le miroir*, pp. 455–62. Efforts in this direction, never truly comprehensive, were the inquests for regulating the taille in 1579, 1583, 1596, and 1600. Chérin, *La noblesse*, pp. 37–41. In 1611 Mayerne called for a general "registre des classes." *La monarchie aristodémocratique*, p. 103. And the idea of official registers showing status was promoted on several occasions between 1614 and 1629 by Claude de Valles. *Mémoires et instructions pour établir en ce royaume un règlement sur le fait des armoiries* (Paris, 1629).

in order that anyone who had complaints might register them. It would then be certified by four old and respected gentilshommes of the region, and individual certificates of status would be distributed to each of the noblemen listed. One copy of the roster would be retained by each of the four old gentilshommes, and one copy filed for reference at the provincial Cour des Aides.[94]

Each individual's official status once thus established, there should be little opportunity for usurpation, for a person would be required to produce his certificate (or a certified copy) whenever he was involved in any legal business. Anyone who called another person "Messire," "Chevalier," or "Escuyer" without first having seen the certificate of status would be guilty of forgery.

The basic problems of noble status were obviously still present in 1614. The anonymous noble's *Discours* was merely one more attempt, albeit worked out with extraordinary thoroughness, to achieve order and clarification.

IV

We have been considering nobility primarily as a legal status. The nobility in France was a privileged class of society, and all kinds of legal questions, such as inheritance, were tied to whether one was inside or outside its boundaries. But it would be wrong to regard noble status exclusively in these terms. For there were other, non-legal criteria of status, such as the willingness of groups to associate on the same level, the extent of intermarriage, the presence or absence of animosities, and other clues to the social conventions and to the hierarchy of prestige within a society.

From this point of view, it is perfectly clear that elaborate theoretical systems and legal rulings did not bridge the gap between old and new nobles. It was all well and good to say that three generations raised one to full noble status, but the person who could trace his status back only this far, or even four or five generations, would still be considered "a new noble," and "would not be held in much respect among the old nobles."[95] There are many indications that the new nobles were not warmly received. At the musters of the ban et arrière-ban, for instance, the old nobles kept themselves "separate and apart" from the anoblis so that they would not be thrown in contact with them during combat.[96]

Particularly intense were the animosities between the old noblesse d'épée and the new noblesse de robe. The former, as Loyseau pointed out, tried to hold themselves apart from the latter, who were trying to merge with them.[97] This trend stretched back for many generations, but it was particularly intense during our period, when there was between these two groups a "perpetual jealousy."[98]

In 1617, at the Assembly of Notables, a typical example of bickering over "precedence" occurred. The leading magistrates claimed that they should be seated in front of the nobility. The nobles were furious. A proposed compromise—having the nobles sit behind the magistrates, but arranging them somehow so that they (or at least some of them) sat close to the king—was unsatisfactory to them. They vehemently insisted that the arrangement was exceptional and would not be followed at the meetings of the Estates General.[99]

In the late sixteenth century, Estienne Pasquier had remarked that the nobility of robe was regarded as bastard by the people.[100] And despite the elaborate explanations of theorists, and the specific legal cases, the view persisted that they were inferior. Marriage between the families of robe and sword was extremely uncommon at the beginning of the seventeenth century.[101]

The significance of the contemporary treatises on noble status should therefore not be exaggerated. In general they are more volitional than descriptive. But they do show that contemporaries were disturbed by the uncertainty and fluidity of social classes. If they were unsuccessful in drawing a sharp line between nobles and roturiers, this was only in part due to poor enforcement and the lax interpretation of prescription. In a larger sense the attempts to strengthen class boundaries were vitiated by the increased social prestige of office-holders and anoblis—a manifestation of the effect of money as a solvent of old distinctions. In the elaborate systems we have examined, some place was almost always provided for the new nobility. This concession was necessary if the proposals were to bear any relationship to reality. But it is a sure sign, also, that any effort to establish a tightly knit, closed caste of privileged nobles was a lost cause.

Conclusion

In the preceding chapters we have examined contemporary views of the French nobility and its role from about 1560 to the ministry of Richelieu. In trying to gain some sense of the tensions and the trends, we have paid little attention to individual writers. The topical approach has required that we consider specific problems instead of focusing on each of the witnesses one by one. I do not wish, at this point, to change the approach, since the Index and the Notes should enable one to discover what these writers had to say, if anything, about the topics treated here. But it is important to ask some biographical questions about our witnesses: What was their class background? What was their profession? Did they hold royal offices? Were they members of one of the Parlements? Were they Catholic or Protestant? In other words, we should not overlook the possibility that their views regarding the nobility may have been influenced by their personal background.[1]

Some of our authorities are well known already: Montaigne, Bodin, Richelieu. Other authorities are "collective"—such as the cahiers, and the pamphlet "by six peasants." In some instances we are faced with pseudonyms or dubious authorship: Crest, Froumenteau, Montand, Vieilleville. And about several of the writers, Ernaud and Froydeville, for example, I have found practically no information. Nevertheless, there may be enough about whom something is known to show whether correlations exist between opinion and religion or class standing.

The number of those with clear credentials of ancient noble background is small. Several of them seem to come from aristocratic families, but either they were of rather recent standing, parvenus of one sort or another, or the age of their noble standing is not readily discoverable. Pierre Brantôme, one of the exceptions, evidently was one of the old nobility; he was raised at the court of Henry II, was named Gentilhomme de la Chambre in 1568, and carried the title of "seigneur et baron de Richemont." Pierre de Boyssat's father was a *vi-bailli* at Vienne, and his older brother was described as "seigneur de Licien"—clues that would lead us to expect noble status. But when we discover that the father was granted a certificate of nobility only in 1602, we realize that this was one of the "new" families. Noël Du Fail was thought of as a nobleman—a country gentleman, according to one source—but he was closely connected to the Parlements, as a judge at Rennes and later as a councillor of the Parlement of Brittany. The same is true of Montaigne, of course, whose noble ancestry we know to be anything but ancient.[2] Others who qualified as nobles in one way or another were Claude Brosse, Guillaume Du Vair, François de La Noue, Guillaume de La Perrière, Gilles-André de La Roque, Blaise de Monluc, and Florentin de Thierriat. Thus much of the discussion with which we have been concerned emanated from the nobility, with a potent strain of the newer or judicial nobles clearly in evidence.

Several of our writers were bourgeois lawyers, jurisconsults, and civil servants, who gave little evidence of considering themselves to be nobles. François de L'Alouëte was a bailli at Vertus before he was made a Conseiller du Roi. Jean Bacquet was an avocat at the Parlement of Paris and at the Chambre des Trésors. Jean Bodin, a professor of law at Toulouse for several years, also filled various offices, including that of

Maître des Requestes. Laurent Bouchel was an avocat at the Parlement of Paris for some forty years. Louis Le Caron, Jean Le Masle, Jacques Leschassier, Charles Loyseau, Estienne Pasquier, François Ragueau—all were lawyers or administrators. But since the road to nobility often ran through the law schools, Parlements, and administrative posts, it is obviously misleading to draw too sharp distinctions of class background.

Although we have included protests from the lower classes, most of the articulated concern came from the nobility itself and from those of the middle class or legal profession who were moving toward nobility.

One might think that the views of contemporary writers would be greatly influenced by their class status. Some of the extreme criticism of the nobility did come from non-nobles resentful of nobles' privileges. But beyond this I find scarcely any correlation of opinions with class status. If some non-nobles wished nobles to be allowed in commerce and industry, some nobles did as well; and opposition to this proposal could be found in both groups, though it may have sprung from different motives. If some non-nobles were critical of the traditional aristocratic contempt for education, several noblemen were arriving at the same conclusion. In advocating changes that would give the nobility a more acceptable rationale for its privileges, nobles and non-nobles often agreed. Outright denunciation of the nobility as a whole or demands for complete abolition of its privileges we do not find coming from noble writers, but then, as we have seen, such extreme views were rare. We are left with various kinds of "moderate" proposals, but the differences among them do not usually lend themselves to a class-interest analysis.

What about religion? Religious background might well have had a bearing on political and social views; indeed, during the age of religious wars it could scarcely be otherwise. We have noticed that in some circles Protestantism had the reputation of being socially equalitarian. Do we, then, find a comparatively radical point of view expressed rather consistently by Protestant writers while Catholics remained staunch defenders of the status quo? Evidence of religious affiliation is frequently lacking, but of those whose religion is known, there are both Protestants and Catholics among our writers. Among the Protestants are Noël Du Fail, Barthélemy de Laffemas, François de La Noue, Pierre de La Place, Louis Regnier de La Planche, La Popelinière, Louis Turquet de Mayerne, and Pierre d'Origny. The Catholics were Pierre de Boyssat, Beroalde de Verville (who abjured his religion at the death of his father), Pierre Brantôme, Jean de Caumont, Pierre Charron, Guy Coquille, Bernard Du Haillan (who converted from Protestantism), Guillaume Du Vair, Michel de L'Hospital, Gilles Le Maistre, Jean Le Masle, Charles Loyseau, Claude de Marois, Blaise de Monluc, Montaigne, Des Osres, Estienne Pasquier, and Maurice Poncet. Those not specified should probably, in the absence of further information, also be assumed to be Catholic.

But, again, there is no discernible correlation between views regarding the nobility and religious faith. Both Protestant and Catholic nobles faced similar problems. The same is true of middle-class lawyers, whose religious affiliation, however it might affect their attitude toward the king during the confused years of the late sixteenth century, did not have any obvious application to the questions we have been considering. There were statements by both Luther and Calvin that could give encouragement to social "levelers," and one cannot rule out the possibility that some French Protestants were influenced by them. But the desire of the leading Reformers to disassociate themselves from social and political radicalism is well known. At the very least, therefore, their influence in France was not all of a kind.

A more fruitful question might very well be whether opinions were influenced by age. Was there a kind of "generation gap," with the writers born after the beginning of the seventeenth century, or those who did not personally remember the religious wars, showing themselves somehow more or

less radical than their fathers? The preliminary searching I
have done in this area fails to show that there was. There was
not unchanging stability of opinion (we have noticed some
kinds of development on specific questions), but judging
from the evidence used here, the generation of one's birth
was not a major determinant of his social views.

In the absence of biographical explanations of opinion regarding the nobility, what is the significance of this study?
Each of the preceding chapters, I hope, speaks for itself in
pointing up one aspect of the nobility's crisis of adjustment.
But perhaps a few final observations are in order.

First, the social awareness and class consciousness of the
period were more intense and more sophisticated than we
might have expected. It is often tempting when considering
the society of a past age to adopt the procedure of George
Bernard Shaw, who put into the mouths of some of his char-
acters words they would have spoken "if they had known
what they were doing." To a surprising extent, the thinkers
of the late sixteenth and early seventeenth centuries did know
what they were doing. Recognizing the social problems of
their generation, they tried to work out solutions to them.

Second, the various problems were interconnected. The ambiguity of noble status was tied up with the diminution of the
nobility's military role, with the theory of dérogeance, and
with the discussion regarding birth and virtue. The anti-noble
sentiment was linked to the desire to rationalize privilege, to
have the nobles perform an accepted social function, and to
require adherence to the moral obligations of noble status.
Since there were several discrepancies to be coped with, and
since various class interests were represented in the debate that
went on for several generations, the programs recommended
sometimes differed widely. Thus, for example, for the nobles
to regain an acceptable social role, some thinkers urged that
they become educated and compete with roturiers. This was
nearly impossible to reconcile with the desire of other writers
to have the nobles remain on their estates, where they would

be in no danger of contamination from mingling with roturiers.

Third, as I hope I have adequately explained in the preceding chapters, the conditions that I have described were not strictly new. One has only to read Elizabeth Salmon Teall's admirable study of the French nobility in the early sixteenth century, Edouard Perroy's and Robert Boutruche's monographs on the fourteenth and fifteenth centuries, and local or regional studies by such historians as Philippe Wolff and Georges Duby to be strongly aware that painful accommodation to new conditions was by no means a new challenge to the French aristocracy. Many of the same problems—incursions of new families, military innovations, administrative reforms favoring middle-class officeholders—can be observed in earlier generations. Admittedly, several of the writers of our period looked back longingly at what appeared to be a kind of "golden age" during the reign of Francis I or before. If we make some allowance for the natural tendency to idealize the past, they did have a point, for the problems faced by the nobility seemed more acute than ever before. But however they viewed the past, the nobles of the age of religious wars were experiencing a set of problems that were not as new as they may have thought.

Fourth, if the present study points back by implication to earlier generations, it also points forward. For the nobility of our period was in many respects the first generation of the nobility of the Old Regime. The major problems associated with the aristocracy of the age of Louis XIV, or of Louis XV, seem clearly discernible at the beginning of the century. Not that the nobility of the Old Regime should be thought of as a cluster of barnacles, for it continued to exert influence, to command respect, and to influence decisions of state. Particularly after the noblesse de robe had become entrenched and had intermarried with the old nobility, the aristocracy as a whole was a class to be reckoned with. The resurgence of the aristocracy in the eighteenth century—marked by vigorous effort to control the highest judicial and military positions and to increase the profits from feudal dues—led to some impressive gains, however temporary. But they were foreshadowed by similar efforts during the late sixteenth and early seventeenth centuries. Indeed, it is only a slight exaggeration to say that the nobility of the Old Regime, from Louis XIV to the French Revolution, reacted to its problems by exploring various solutions that had been vigorously debated during the earlier period. For the fundamental dilemma of the French nobility—how to be economically prosperous yet aloof from economic involvements, how to perform a recognized social role deserving of privilege while resisting pressure to redefine classes according to actual service, how to maintain the pride and tradition of an hereditary aristocracy while seeing character attributes as something more than an "entailed inheritance," how, in short, to put forth a convincing rationale of class privilege based on both service and distinctiveness—had been argued and reargued during the tumultuous period from the age of religious wars to the ministry of Richelieu.

Notes

Notes

NOTES TO INTRODUCTION

1. Lucien Romier, *Le royaume de Catherine de Médicis* (Paris, 1921), I, 169–75; Henri Hauser, *La prépondérance espagnole,* 3d ed. (Paris, 1948), pp. 203–9.

2. As quoted in Hauser, *La prépondérance espagnole,* p. 204.

3. On the nobility's economic plight, see François de La Noue, *Discours politiques et militaires* (n.p., 1612), p. 157; see also pp. 15, 32, 51–52, 93, 96. The first edition of this work was published in 1587. Of the many contemporary references to the economic condition of the nobility, two other examples are *Le paysan françois* (n.p., n.d.), and Louis Musset, *Discours sur les rémontrances et réformation de chacun état* (Paris, 1582), p. 73.

4. Current scholarship on the question of the nobility's economic decline is examined in the essay on pp. 168–74.

5. See Henri Hauser, "La crise de 1557–1559 et le bouleversement des fortunes," in *Mélanges Lefranc* (Paris, 1936), pp. 307–19; and Romier, *Le royaume de Catherine de Médicis,* I, 178–79, 197.

6. La Noue, *Discours,* pp. 51–52.

7. Maurice Weiler, *La pensée de Montaigne* (Paris, 1948), p. 111.

8. "Icy me voila engagé à une matière fort commune, n'y en ayant possible aucune du droict François, qui ait esté traittée par plus d'autheurs, que celle de la Noblesse, dont les Philosophes moraux, les politiques, les humanistes, les Jurisconsultes, voire encore les practiciens modernes, ont escrit chacun à sa mode." Charles Loyseau, *Ordres,* ch. V, para. 1, in *Oeuvres* (Lyon, 1701).

NOTES TO CHAPTER I

1. The violence in Brittany, as elsewhere, was often based on religious differences or political factions. But the undercurrent of class hostility becomes evident when we read that the peasants wished to kill even the nobles within their own party. Jean Moreau, *Histoire de ce qui est passé en Bretagne durant les guerres de la Ligue* (Saint-Brieuc, 1857), pp. 16,

88, 95–101, 108–12, 386, 395–97; Edmond Durtelle de Saint-Sauveur, *Histoire de Bretagne* (Rennes, 1957), II, 62–64.

2. It was the nobles of Guienne who feared being forced into servitude. *Mémoires de Condé*, ed. Secousse (London, 1743), III, 107–11. Those who wanted to treat the nobles "à la façon de Suisse" were mentioned by La Noue, *Discours politiques et militaires*, p. 87; by Guillaume de La Perrière, *Le miroir politique contenant diverses manières de gouverner et policer les républiques* (Paris, 1567), p. 32; and by François de L'Alouëte, *Des affaires d'estat, des finances, du prince et de sa noblesse* (Metz, 1597), p. 218. The desire of some to "exterminate" the nobles is mentioned by La Noue, *Discours*, p. 87. Also by L'Alouëte, *Affaires,* p. 165: "Ne void-on pas qu-on ne cherche que de les exterminer tous les jours?" For other examples of the nobles' fear of the peasants, see Claude Haton, *Mémoires*, ed. F. Bourquelot (Paris, 1857), I, 333–34, 712. Roland Mousnier has pointed out that the later revolts, of 1623–48, were often led by nobles against rich officeholders. Nevertheless, peasant hatred of the nobility was one element in the total picture. Roland Mousnier, "Recherches sur les soulèvements populaires en France avant la Fronde," *Revue d'histoire moderne et contemporaine,* V (1958), 81–113.

3. David Du Rivault de Flurance, *Les états, esquels il est discouru du prince, du noble, et du tiers estat* (Lyon, 1596), p. 257.

4. Lalourcé and Duval, eds., *Recueil des cahiers généraux des trois ordres aux états généraux* (Paris, 1789), I, 314–17.

5. Hugues Imbert, "Les Grands Jours de Poitiers: Registres criminels," in *Mém. soc. de statistique ... des Deux-Sèvres*, 2e sér., XVI (1878).

6. Henri Sée, *Les états de Bretagne au XVIᵉ siècle* (1895), p. 52; Maurice de Bengi-Puyvallée, "Extraits des cahiers des assemblées du tiers état du duché de Berry en 1576 et 1588," *Mém. des antiquaires du Centre* (1934–35), p. 147.

7. Lalourcé and Duval, eds., *Cahiers,* I, p. 318.

8. La Noue, *Discours*, p. 13; see also pp. 65, 88, 105–6.

9. "Quant aux gentilshommes & à la Noblesse, elle nous est aujourd'huy le plus souvent onereuse & quelquefois insupportable, principalement à nous autres paisans, au lieu que leur vray exercice & vacation seroit nous conserver & soulager, il leur faut toujours quelque corvée, le plus beau de nos cochons, quelque septier d'avoyne, quelque chartée de foin ou paille, autrement nous sommes menacez de gensdarmes; & si la guerre peut retourner (laquelle plusieurs d'entr'eux souhaittent, aussi bien que nostre beaux Soldat François, s'ennuyent de la paix) l'on apprendra à ces pieds gris (disent-ils de nous) à respecter autrement la noblesse. Tantost un de nous est bastonné pour avoir manqué d'aller charroyer pour Monsieur; l'autre pour n'avoir salué de tout loing Ma-

damoiselle, & ne s'estre levé devant elle quand elle entre en l'Eglise, ou ne lui avoir fact le pied de veau quand elle passe: l'autre pour n'avoir voulu vendre sa terre ou sa vigne à leur mot, sera menacé qu'on lui coupera les jarets: à l'autre l'on mariera sa fille contre son gré à quelque cuisinier ou cocher de monsieur, s'il a si gros train, sinon à son palfrenier ou laquais: & quand il veut faire chasser, faut que nous autres pauvres sujets nous y allions par bandes avec arbalestes, fourches, & besaces, si nous voulons manger (car l'on ne nous donneroit pas seulement un verre d'eau) autrement nous serions battus ou mulctez d'amende." Anon., *Le paysan françois* (n.p., [c. 1614]), pp. 16–17.

10. Regnier de La Planche, *Histoire de l'estat de France*, ed. Mennechet (Paris, 1836), p. 302.

11. "En temps de paix, les gentilshommes, tant d'ung que de l'aultre parti, ne sont gueres estudiens de la sincerité de la justice.... Plusieurs voleries, murdres se sont commys et commectent à le terre des gentilhommes; lesquelz passent tout par connivence et sans punition, et sovent retirent chez eux les délinquens, et euxmesmes commectent infinies concussions sur leurs subjectz; lesquelz, si s'en veullent pleindre devant les seneschaux pour estre sauvegardés, reçoivent tant de mavays traictement par de personnes interposes, que le pouvre subject en demeure ruyné et sa familhe; de quoy avons infinis exemples. Et quant à l'execution des ordonnances de la justice du Roy données contre aucuns gentilshommes, il est notoire que plusieurs d'iceulx possedent de bénéfices et héritages d'aultruy contre les sentences des sénéschaux et arrestz de la court, pour l'exécution desquelz arretz il n'y a aucun huissier, sergent, ni aultre officier roial qu'ausat prendre exploicter aucunes lettres contre lesdits gentilshommes, de peur d'estre battu." Célestin Douais, ed., *Mémoires sur l'état du clergé, de la noblesse, de la justice, et du peuple dans les diocèses de Narbonne, de Montpellier et de Castres en 1573* (Toulouse, 1891), p. 44.

12. Imbert, in *Mèm. soc. de statistique ... des Deux-Sèvres*, p. 122.

13. For specific instances, see *ibid.*, pp. 128–29, 131, 132ff, 161, 176, 184f. Similar incidents had occurred in 1567. *Ibid.*, pp. 63–64, 70, 72–73, 101, 107. See also Nicolas de Montand (pseud.), *Le miroir des françois* (n.p., 1581), pp. 84–85. Edicts against the excesses can be found in François-André Isambert, *et al.*, *Recueil général des anciennes lois françaises* (Paris, 1833), XIV, 266, 445ff, 486.

14. Nicolas de Crest (pseud.), *Le cabinet du roy de France, dans lequel il y a trois perles precieuses* (Paris, 1581), pp. 315–16, 322.

15. Estienne Pasquier, *Oeuvres* (Amsterdam, 1723), II, 178.

16. Bernard de Girard, Seigneur Du Haillan, *De l'estat et succez des affaires de France* (Paris, 1570), p. 81. Du Haillan tended, in this edition especially, to rely on theory and books rather than observation.

17. Du Haillan, *De l'estat*, rev. ed., 1611, p. 173.

18. *Advis, remonstrances et requestes aux estats généraux tenus à Paris, 1614* (n.p., n.d.). Par six paysans.

19. Haton enjoys a bad pun, but this should not obscure the essential point he is making. The rebels, he says, were "pour la plus part gentils-hommes, ou, pour mieux dire, gens pillehommes." *Mémoires*, I, 333–34. Compare this with his observation ten years later: "Les genstue-hommes sont gens pillehommes en plusieurs endroictz de ce royaume, et n'ont rien en plus grande hayne que leurs subjectz ... et par tous les moyens licites et illicites s'emploient à leur faire perdre leurs biens et les attribuent à eux par force, audace de coups de baston et corruption de justice." *Ibid.*, II, 712.

20. Douais, ed., *Mémoires sur l'état du clergé*, p. 27. Cf. the complaints from Agenais, in 1588, of the "grand connivance et frequentation que la noblesse ou la pluspart de celle dudict pays faict avec lesdicts enemys." Georges Tholin, "Des tailles et des impositions au pays d'Agenais durant le XVIᵉ siècle," *Recueil des travaux de la soc. d'agric., sciences et arts d'Agen,* 2d series, IV (1875), 9.

21. Eustache Piémond, *Mémoires*, ed. J. Brun-Durand (Valence, 1885), pp. 216, 246, 267.

22. Baron de Fourquevaux, "Discours au roy du comportement de ses sujets," in Vaissette, *Histoire générale de Languedoc*, XII, 1071.

23. Douais, ed., *Mémoires sur l'état du clergé*, p. 27.

24. L'Alouëte, *Affaires*, p. 217.

25. Anon., *Les escriptures et deffences des gents de la noblesse de Dauphiné* (Lyon, c. 1595), pp. 10–11.

26. Fernand Fleuret and Louis Perceau, eds., *Les satires françaises du XVIᵉ siècle* (Paris, 1922), p. 70.

27. *Ibid.*, p. 109.

28. *Ibid.*, pp. 152–53.

29. *Ibid.*, pp. 107–8.

30. *Ibid.*, p. 229.

31. Raoul Chandon de Briailles and Henri Bertal, eds., *Archives municipales d'Epernay: XVIᵉ siècle* (Paris, 1906), p. 157.

32. Imbert, in *Mém. soc. de statistique ... des Deux-Sèvres*, p. 122.

33. Johan Huizinga, *The Waning of the Middle Ages* (New York, 1954), p. 58.

34. Cardin Le Bret, "Sur l'anoblissement d'une métaire roturière en Bretagne; & que cela ne s'est pû faire sans indemniser la paroisse où elle est assise," in *Oeuvres*, rev. ed. (Paris, 1688), pp. 538–40.

35. *Ibid.*, p. 113.

36. Chandon de Briailles and Bertal, *Archives municipales d'Eper-nay*, p. 157.

37. Anon., *Lettre missive d'un gentilhomme à un sien compagnon,*

contenant les causes du mescontentement de la noblesse de France (n.p., 1567), no pagination.

38. In 1614, answering the demand that taxes be reduced, Louis XIII said that this could be done by "subjecting to the taille five or six thousand of the exempt, who avoid paying the taille by a thousand means, although they are liable and for the most part rich and opulent." Ch. J. de Mayer, *Des états généraux et autres assemblées nationales* (Paris, 1789), XVI, 29.

39. Proposals for a *taxe unique sur les feux* cropped up several times —in 1576, 1588, and 1597—in connection with meetings of the Estates General or of the Assembly of Notables. [G.M.R.] Picot, *Histoire des états généraux* (Paris, 1872), I, 495ff; III, 12, 197, 317–19.

40. *Lettre missive d'un gentilhomme.*

41. Lalourcé and Duval, eds., *Cahiers*, I, in article 14 of the Second Estate's first cahier.

42. La Lande de Calan, ed., *Documents inédits relatifs aux états de Bretagne, 1491–1589* (Rennes, 1908–9), II, 59. Deciding who were "truly nobles" was itself no easy matter. See Chapter 6.

43. *Ibid.,* II, 119.

44. *Ibid., I*, 222.

45. For a discussion of the complexities of taille réelle, see Edmond Esmonin, *Etudes sur la France des XVIIᵉ et XVIIIᵉ siècles* (Paris, 1964), pp. 167–74.

46. Lalourcé and Duval, eds., *Recueil des pièces originales et authentiques concernant la tenue des états généraux* (Paris, 1789), II, 106.

47. Montand, *Le miroir,* p. 459.

48. Anon., *La iuste plaincte et remonstrance faicte au roy . . . par le pauvre peuple de Daulphiné* (Lyon, 1597), p. 15.

49. *Ibid.,* p. 34.

50. Anon., *La responce du tiers estat et commun peuple aux escriptures du second estat & gents de la noblesse de Daulphiné* (Lyon, 1595), pp. 8, 9.

51. *La iuste plaincte,* p. 40.

52. *La responce du tiers estat,* p.18.

53. Anon., *Les escriptures,* pp. 12–13.

54. *La responce du tiers estat,* p. 10.

55. *Ibid.,* p. 21.

56. *Ibid.,* p. 18.

57. L'Abbé A. Dussert, "Catherine de Médicis et les états du Dauphiné," *Bulletin de l'académie delphinale,* 6th ser., II, (1931), 132.

58. *Les escriptures,* p. 7.

59. *Ibid.,* p. 12.

60. *La responce du tiers estat*, p. 9. The pamphlet quotes or para-phrases some of the opposing arguments before answering them.

61. For some examples of the intimate relations between lords and peasants, see Henri Baudrillart, *Gentilshommes ruraux de la France* (Paris, 1894); Pierre de Vaissiere, *Gentilshommes campagnards de l'ancienne France*, 2d ed. (Paris, 1925); and Elizabeth S. Teall, "The Seigneur of Renaissance France: Advocate or Oppressor?" *Journal of Modern History*, Vol. XXXVII, No. 2 (1965), 131–50.

62. The roturiers, having noticed that they were richer than many nobles, "ont sur ce batti des desseins plus outriers." Some of them, "en rompant les barrières de leur condition et estat plebee [cherchent] à s'eslever et inserer en l'estat de la noblesse." Others simply noticed that poor nobles were considered above them: "De là ils viennent butter à ceste maxime, que Nature nous a faits esgaux.... Et prisans fort leur opulence, mesprisent à l'esgal la povreté de la Noblesse." *La responce du tiers estat*, p. 9.

63. Le Bret, *Oeuvres*, p. 62.

64. Louis Turquet de Mayerne, *Apologie contre les destracteurs de livres de la monarchie aristodémocratique* (Paris, 1611), p. 241. May-erne's views are discussed by Roland Mousnier in "L'Opposition politi-que bourgeoise à la fin du XVIe et au début du XVIIe siècle," *Revue historique*, CCXIII (1955), 1–20.

65. The details of the dispute, which it would be tedious to retrace here, can be found in Mayer, *Des états généraux*, XVI, 203ff and, es-pecially, 223–28.

66. Anon., *Chasse au vieil grognard de l'antiquité* (1622), reprinted by Edouard Fournier in *Variétés historiques et littéraires* (Paris, 1855–63), III, 27–66.

67. L'Alouëte, *Affaires*, p. 218.

68. Du Rivault, *Les états*, p. 245; see also pp. 251, 253, 255, 257.

69. *Mémoires de Condé*, III, 108–11.

70. Anon., *Advertissement envoyé à la noblesse de France, tant du parti du roy, que des rebelles & coniurez* (Paris, 1574).

71. *Ibid.*

72. *Lettres de monseigneur le cardinal Caietan ... envoyées à la noblesse de France* (Lyon, 1590), pp. 5–6.

NOTES TO CHAPTER 2

1. N. Tommaseo, ed., *Rélations des ambassadeurs vénetiens sur les affaires de France* (1838), I, 491.

2. Lalourcé and Duval, eds., *Recueil des cahiers généraux des trois ordres aux états généraux*, II, 70, 122, 283.

3. Montaigne, *Essays*, tr. Trechmann (New York and London, n.d.), Bk. II, ch. 7.

4. Loyseau, *Ordres*, ch. 5, para. 80, in *Oeuvres*.

5. For a discussion of the ban et arrière-ban, with bibliography, see Roger Doucet, *Les institutions de la France au XVI⁰ siècle* (Paris, 1948), II, 610–19; and Gaston Zeller's one-volume work of the same title (Paris, 1948), pp. 312–14. Also useful for general purposes is Pierre Lebeurier, *Rôle des taxes de l'arrière-ban du bailliage d'Evreux en 1562* (Paris, 1861).

6. On the difficulty with which impoverished noblemen supported the burden of the ban et arrière-ban, see Romier, *Le royaume de Catherine de Médicis*, I, 178–79.

7. That contemporaries occasionally recognized some of the complex social changes underlying the demise of the ban et arrière-ban is suggested by the following observation from Dauphiny: "C'est chose presque impossible de tirer le service, & soulagement que doit se rendre ledit Arrière-ban; d'autant que les Officiers, & Nobles de robbe longue s'en disent exemps: à quoy il leur est facile de se maintenir, tant par l'authorité de leurs charges, qu'à cause de leur vocation, qui rend leurs personnes inhabiles audit effect: cependant ils font & composent la plus grand partie des Nobles de la province, & y possedent le plus des biens: ce qui fait que tous les autres perdent la volonté de faire leur devoir, voyans la plus grand part, & les plus riches en estre exemps." Anon., *Cayer presenté au roy par ceux du tiers estat de Dauphiné* (Grenoble, 1619), pp. 4–5.

8. Zeller, *Les institutions de la France au XVI⁰ siècle*, p. 314. Cf. Ferdinand Lot, *Recherches sur les effectifs des armées françaises . . . 1492–1562* (Paris, 1962), pp. 138ff.

9. "Le ban et arrière ban desdites séneschaussées de Toulouse & Lauraguez souloient représenter au roy en ses affaires quelques centaines d'hommes d'armes, avec leur suite d'archers: tout cela fut alteré & abatardi par la commutation que fust faitte du temps du roy François le Grand, de gens bien montés & armés, qu'ils estoient ou devoient estre, en gens de pied. Il n'y a quasi rien de ce temps dont faille faire estime, & le plus pauvre gentilhomme se mesprise de respondre audit arrière ban." Baron de Fourquevaux, "Discours au roy du comportement de ses sujets," in Vaissette, *Histoire générale de Languedoc*, XII, 1075.

10. "Aux montres des arrierebans, estoient les gentilshommes d'ancienne race separez et à part, qui, pour mourir, n'eussent souffert que les annoblis ou autres ayans permission acquerir fiefs nobles, qui estoient en autre bande et regiment, se fussent joints et approchez d'eux au combat, afin et pour ne confondre la vaillance des uns avec le bas coeur et inexperience des autres. Ce qui a fait qu'en ce jour les arrierebans,

composez de valets des nobles, qui dedaignent, peu exceptez, marcher avec ces sentans encore, la charrue et boutique, ne valent plus qu'a doubleure, comme ne rendans aucun combattant; se que nous avons veu arriver de nostre temps." Noël Du Fail, *Contes et discours d'Eutrapel* (Paris, 1875), II, 41.

11. "On la trouvera de nul service ne proffit: car ce n'est autre chose que le service de cent hommes d'armes en cas de nécessité dans le pays, ou hors d'iceluy pour la deffence dudict pays durant quarante jours. Si bien qu'avant que la levée en soit accordée, sur laquelle on contredict bien souvent, ou avant que la perequation soit faicte pour le payment, & solde, ou que la soulde soit exigée, ou que les personnes qui doyvent servir soyent esleües & nommées, comme l'on a accoustumé, toute occasion de bien faire se perd, ou plustost toute la necessité se passe, ou bien l'entreprise est delaissée imparfaicte, le temps de quarante jours finy." Anon., *La responce du tiers estat et commun peuple aux escriptures du second estat & gents de la noblesse de Daulphiné*, pp. 23, 28.

12. Lebeurier lists the following convocations of the ban et arrière-ban in the late sixteenth century: 1551, 1552, 1553, 1554, 1555, 1557, 1558, 1562, 1567, 1568, 1569, 1575, and 1587. *Rôle des taxes*, pp. 36-40. They were mostly local levies and, as La Noue indicates, the financial return was the main objective. La Noue, *Discours politiques et militaires*, pp. 227-29, 232.

13. On the general significance of the decline of the ban et arrière-ban, a French historian has recently said that "sans nul doute, le souvenir subsiste de la chevalerie guerrière: les nobles sont des soldats, les premiers du royaume; mais s'ils ne répondent plus à l'appel du roi convoquant le ban et l'arrière-ban—ce qui s'est verifié maintes fois, et notamment en 1575 et en 1635—c'est qu'ils ont perdu le sens de leur devoir militaire." Robert Mandrou, *Introduction à la France moderne, 1500-1640: Essai de psychologie historique* (Paris, 1961), p. 144.

14. The number of Swiss soldiers in the service of France fluctuated between 10,000 and 19,000 until it was reduced by a treaty in 1549, which stated that the number would remain between 6,000 and 16,000. Doucet, *Les institutions*, II, 636.

15. Charles de Robillard de Beaurepaire, "Etat de l'armée française en 1552," *Bull. de la soc. de l'hist. de Normandie* (1883), III, 229-32. See also Lot, *Recherches sur les effectifs des armées françaises*, pp. 125ff. For a general discussion of the decline of heavy cavalry, see Charles Oman, *A History of the Art of War in the Sixteenth Century* (New York, 1937), pp. 33ff, 227.

16. François de Vieilleville, *Mémoires* (Paris, 1757), pp. 128-29. It has been shown that this work is a forgery, but it reflects the conditions and attitudes of the time.

17. Le Bret, *Oeuvres*, p. 485.

18. Tommaseo, ed., *Rélations des ambassadeurs vénetiens*, II, 198.

19. Isambert, *Recueil général des anciennes lois françaises*, XIV, 54.

20. Guy Coquille, *Oeuvres* (Paris, 1666), I, 257, 311.

21. "Et pour abastardir encores davantage le coeur de la Noblesse, quand quelques compagnies de gensdarmes ont vacqué, au lieu d'en gratifier ceux qui avoyent si bien servi aux guerres furieuses, contre ce grand Empereur Charles, ou bien en recompenser ceux, à qui illegitemement on avoit osté leurs charges, les ont baillees, aucunes à des enfans de Presidens de Paris, les autres à des gens qui n'avoyent jamais bougé des bordeaux dudict Paris, ou des environs: autres qui ne commanderent jamais qu'à leurs valets, Gentilshommes comme eux, ou à tout le moins à des tailleurs, chaussetiers, peintres, brodeurs, & autres personnes de mestier de garderobe: & autres qu'on tien bien de race de gentilshommes, mais si peu exercez aux afaires de la guerre, que le plus habille ne sauroit faire la moindre faction qui appartienne à un soldat." Anon., *Lettre missive d'un gentilhomme à un sien compagnon, contenant les causes du mescontentement de la noblesse de France*, no pagination.

22. "As tu opinion qu'on puisse tirer service en la militie de France lors qu'elle sera remplie de personnes de vil estat, non duits ny exercites aux armes, & que meriteroient mieux d'estre au rang des pirates & escumiers de mer, ou des bandoliers qui sont aux montagnes de Foix & autres lieux circonvoisins que de se parangonner du tiltre de gendarme, qui est un injure manifestement faicte à nos devanciers, & aux gentilshommes qui sont extraicts de noble & ancienne race, lesquels sont constraints de se rendre pair & compagnons de gens de basse condition & de petite valeur. Voilà d'où vient tant de noises & debats qu'on void maintenant en ce Royaume. Voilà d'ou vient que la gendarmerie n'est pas payée comme elle souloit, c'est la cause qui fait souvent fuir & gaigner la garite aux plus vaillans capitaines de nostre France, qui par faute de gens de coeur & d'honneur n'oseroient faire teste s'ils sont chargez de l'ennemy, car pensant avoir des hommes ils ont des effeminez, cuidant avoir des nobles ils ont des villains." Montand, *Le miroir des françois*, pp. 132ff.

23. Blaise de Monluc, *Commentaires*, ed. Paul Courteault (Paris, 1911–25), III, 376, 389, 390.

24. Lebeurier, *Rôle des taxes*, pp. 40–41.

25. La Noue, *Discours*, discourse 14. Since nobles historically had not served in the infantry, La Noue must have been contrasting what he saw with an idealized picture of an infantry of noblemen.

26. Vieilleville, *Mémoires*, pp. 128–29.

27. Zeller, *Les institutions*, p. 299.

28. *La responce du tiers estat*, p. 37.

29. "Pour avoir receu un petit coup en la bataille de Coutras il n'a plus voulu depuis manger de la guerre, ny retourner aux armées, mais seulement pour dire qu'il est du mestier, il se contente de porter une queue de poisle...s'aydant des commoditez de la guerre sans en souffrir les incommoditez." Anon., *Le paysan françois* (n.p., n.d.), p. 127.

30. As quoted in André Lacroix, *Claude Brosse et les tailles* (Valence, 1899), p. 43.

31. Lalourcé and Duval, eds., *Cahiers*, I, p. 49.

32. La Lande de Calan, ed., *Documents inédits*, I, 219.

33. Maurice de Bengi-Puyvallée, "Extraits des cahiers des assemblées du tiers état du duché de Berry en 1576 et 1588," *Mém. des antiquaires du Centre* (1934–35), p. 147.

34. "Et par ce que les charges antiennes de ban et arriere-ban sont comme esteintes et abolies a cause que Vostre Majeste dresse ses armes par ses capitaines et gouverneurs de provinces aux despens du peuple, sur lequel a ses fins le talhon est par expres leve, ils vous plaira de vouloire cottizer en deniers les seigneuries et biens nobles subjetz audict ban et arriere ban dont ilz ne payent aucun devoir, et ce a proportion des charges et services qu'ilz sont tenus de prester et randre, a raison desquelz ilz sont taxes au ban et arriere-ban, et que cella soit destine au payement de la gendarmerie, et, ce faict, que la talhon, dont le paouvre peuble est extremement foule, soit suprime et aboly." Tholin, *Cahier des doléances du tiers état du pays d'Agenais aux états généraux* (Paris, 1885), pp. 44–45.

35. Vicomte Oscar de Poli, *Essai d'introduction à l'histoire généalogique* (Paris, 1887), p. 21.

36. La Noue, *Discours*, pp. 225ff.

37. Isambert, *Recueil général*, XIII, 41.

38. *Ibid.*, XIV, 442, 450.

39. *Les basiliques ou édicts et ordonnances de roys de France* (1611), p. 374.

40. Isambert, *Recueil général*, XV, 21, 37; Le Bret, *Oeuvres*, pp. 440–42; L.N.H. Chérin, *Abrégé chronologique d'édits, declarations, règlements, arrêts et lettres patentes...*, in J.-P. Migne, *Nouvelle encyclopédie théologique*, Vol. XIII (Paris, 1861).

41. Cardinal de Richelieu, *Maximes d'état ou testament politique*, ed. Louis André (Paris, 1947), ch. IX, sec. 4.

42. Crest, *Le cabinet du roy de France, dans lequel il y a trois perles precieuses*, 2d ed. (n.p., 1582), pp. 288, 373, 448, 455.

43. Anon., *La vérité des justes defences de la noblesse du Dauphiné* (c. 1599), p. 82; anon., *Advis au roy...des moyens de bannir le luxe*

du royaume, d'establir un grand nombre de manufactures en iceluy
(n.p., 1614), pp. 23, 37.

44. Letter in Estienne Pasquier, *Oeuvres*, II, 1129.

45. Pierre de Bourdeilles, Seigneur de Brantôme, *Oeuvres complètes*, ed. Lalanne (Paris, 1864–82), V, 367–68.

46. Monluc, *Commentaires*, I, 101–2.

47. *Essays*, tr. Trechmann, Bk. II, ch. 17. A marginal addition made by Montaigne after 1588.

48. Le Bret, *Oeuvres*, p. 485.

49. Isambert, *Recueil général*, XIV, 541, 545. Florentin de Thierriat, *Trois traités; de la noblesse de race, de la noblesse civile & des immunitez des ignobles* (Paris, 1606), pp. 326–27, discusses the effect on status of serving in the ordnance companies.

50. Le Bret, *Oeuvres*, p. 485.

51. The language of this later edict (1603) was very close to that of 1583: the ennoblement was "fors & excepté toutesfois . . . ceux aussi qui indeuëment contreviennent à nos Ordonnances, & qui de leur nature estans taillables, se sont de plein saut mis en nosdites ordonnances sans premier avoir fait aucun exercise des armes en autres charges." Louis Le Caron, *Pandectes ou digestes du droict françois*, rev. ed. (Paris, 1637), edicts, 4. Sir Robert Dallington remarked that exemption from the taille was enjoyed by all *gendarmes* and all military officers. *The View of Fraunce, 1604* (Oxford, 1936; facsimile reprint of 1604 ed.), p. 127.

52. Brantôme, *Oeuvres complètes*, V, 383.

53. Lalourcé and Duval, eds., *Cahiers*, II, 72.

54. Anon., *Discours d'un gentilhomme françois à la noblesse de France, sur l'ouverture de l'assemblée des états généraux dans la ville de Paris en ceste année 1614* (n.p., n.d.), p. 7.

55. André Tiraqueau, *Tractatus de nobilitate* (Paris, 1549), ch. 8.

56. Thierriat, *Trois traités*, pp. 155–56; also pp. 148, 328–29.

57. Marcel de La Bigne de Villeneuve, although perhaps too sweeping, was probably not far from the truth when he said that "until the end of the Old Regime the nobles did not cease to fulfill their military obligations, if not to the same extent as originally, as least in a strong enough fashion." *Essai sur la théorie de la dérogeance de la noblesse considérée dans ses rapports avec la constitution sociale de l'ancienne France* (Rennes, 1918), p. 51.

NOTES TO CHAPTER 3

1. The lack of a recognized social function for the nobility is described in Romier, *Le royaume de Catherine de Médicis*, I, 170–73.

2. "Le roi a enlevé aux seigneurs la plupart des affaires lucratives; des causes qui leur restent, le profit est minime." Imbart de La Tour, *Les origines de la Réforme*, I, 396.

3. Some evidence can be found in F. Dumont, "La noblesse et les états particuliers français," in *Etudes presentées à la commission internationale pour l'hist. des assemblées d'états* (Louvain, 1952), p. 152; and in Noël Valois, *Le Conseil du Roi aux XIVe, XVe, et XVIe siècles*, pp. 162–63, 172, 177.

4. Mandrou, *Introduction à la France moderne: Essai de psychologie historique, 1500–1640* (Paris, 1961), p. 146. For details see Doucet, *Les institutions de la France au XVIe siècle*, I, 167–228.

5. Monluc, as quoted by Agénor Bardoux, *Les légistes, leur influence sur la société française* (Paris, 1877), p. 118.

6. Anon., *La vérité des justes defences de la noblesse du Dauphiné*, pp. iii, 8.

7. Anon., *Lettre missive d'un gentilhomme à un sien compagnon, contenant les causes du mescontentement de la noblesse de France.*

8. Anon., *Response à une lettre escrite à Compiegne du quatrième jour d'aoust, touchant le mescontentement de la noblesse de France.*

9. *Lettre missive d'un gentilhomme.*

10. Eymar de Froydeville, *Dialogues de l'origine de la noblesse* (Lyon, 1574), p. 79.

11. Pierre de Boyssat, *Remerciement au roy par les annoblis du Dauphiné, où il est touché de la dignité de la noblesse* (Paris, 1603), pp. 13–14.

12. In Estienne Pasquier, *Oeuvres*, II, 1072, 1129.

13. Pierre de La Place, *Traitè de la vocation et manière de vivre à laquelle chacun est appellé* (Paris, 1561), pp. 59–60.

14. Jean Bodin, *Six livres de la république* (Paris, 1576), livre VI, ch. 6.

15. *Ibid.*

16. Julien Peleus, *Oeuvres* (Paris, 1638), pp. 371–74.

17. Gaspard de Saulx-Tavannes, *Mémoires*, I, 97, as quoted in Louis Wolff, *La vie des parlementaires provençaux au XVIe siècle* (n.p., 1924), pp. 11–12.

18. Dallington, *View of Fraunce*. Nicolas de Crest, Noël Du Fail, Bernard Du Haillan, Claude Fauchet, and Vincent de La Loupe all deplored the nobility's lack of education.

19. As quoted in Wolff, *La vie des parlementaires*, pp. 11–12.

20. Claude Fauchet, *Antiquitez gauloises et françoises*, pp. 336–37 in *Oeuvres* (Paris, 1610). L'Alouëte stated that ignorance of letters was responsible for the common failure of nobles to keep accurate genea-

logical records. *Traité des nobles et des vertus dont ils sont formez* (Paris, 1577), p. 73.

21. Froydeville, *Dialogues*, p. 42.

22. L'Alouëte, *Des affaires d'estat, des finances, du prince et de sa noblesse*, pp. 166ff. Although my references here are to the 1597 work, the section on nobility seems to be unchanged from the earlier *Traité des nobles* (1577).

23. *Ibid.*, p. 169.

24. *Ibid.*, pp. 170–71.

25. *Ibid.*, pp. 171–72.

26. *Ibid.*, p. 173.

27. Pierre d'Origny, *Le hérault de la noblesse de France* (Lyon, 1578). His plan is described on p. 39. The idea of a special noble academy was not original with Origny, who knew of a similar unfulfilled project of Francis I.

28. *Ibid.*, pp. 38–41.

29. Du Rivault, *Les états, esquels il est discouru du prince, du noble, et du tiers estat,* p. 355; see also pp. 216, 219–21.

30. Anon., *La vraye noblesse* (Lyon, 1599), p. 14, as cited in Maurice Magendie, *La politesse mondaine et les théories d'honnêteté en France au XVIIᵉ siècle* (Paris, 1925), I, 341–42.

31. Thierriat, *Trois traités; de la noblesse de race, de la noblesse civile & des immunitez des ignobles,* p. 35.

32. *Ibid.*, pp. 32–34.

33. *Ibid.*, p. 45.

34. *Ibid.*, pp. 41–42.

35. *Ibid.*, pp. 37–38.

36. Mayerne, *La monarchie aristodémocratique*, preface.

37. For a modern study of Mayerne as an advocate of a *noblesse de mérites*, see Roland Mousnier, "L'opposition politique bourgeoise à la fin du XVIᵉ et au début du XVIIᵉ siècle," *Revue historique,* CCXIII (1955), 1–20.

38. Mayerne, *La monarchie aristodémocratique*.

39. *Le paysan françois,* according to a book dealer's notation, is a "livre d'un très grande rareté, publié à l'occasion des Etats-Généraux de 1614 et non cité dans les bibliographies ou catalogues."

40. *Ibid.*, p. 134.

41. *Ibid.*, 128.

42. "Ces lettres & estudes pour estre poenibles, longues, & de coust, ayant esté quitees par la noblesse, il luy a esté necessaire quand & quand de quitter la place des charges publiques & offices aux roturiers, d'autant que ne se trouvant plus de personnes de nobles race qui voulus-

sent prendre la peine d'estudier, afin de se rendre capables & suffisantes pour exercer telles charges, les roturiers ont sceu prendre l'occasion par les cheveux, & se servant de la necessité, se sont introduicts aux offices & dignitez, & en fin se sont faicts rechercher pour les tenir." *Ibid.*, pp. 128–29.

43. *Ibid.*, pp. 136–37.

44. *Ibid.*, p. 139.

45. *Ibid.*, p. 130.

46. *Ibid.*, pp. 139–40.

47. *Advis, remonstrances et requestes aux estats generaux tenus à Paris, 1614.* Par six paysans.

48. *Ibid.*, p. 34.

49. *Ibid.*, p. 22.

50. Anon., *Discours d'un gentilhomme françois à la noblesse de France, sur l'ouverture de l'assemblée des états généraux dans la ville de Paris en ceste année 1614.*

51. *Ibid.*, pp. 9–10.

52. *Ibid.*, p. 8.

53. *Ibid.*, p. 10.

54. *Ibid.*, pp. 60–62.

55. *Ibid.*, pp. 60–62.

56. *Ibid.*, p. 62.

57. Lalourcé and Duval, eds., *Recueil des cahiers généraux des trois ordres aux états généraux,* I, 136.

58. *Ibid.*, II, 136.

59. Picot, *Histoire des états généraux,* III, 174, 178–80.

60. Lalourcé and Duval, eds., *Cahiers,* I, 148.

61. *Ibid.*, II, 146.

62. *Ibid.*

63. *Ibid.*, I, 253.

64. *Ibid.*, I, 159.

65. Picot, *Histoire des états généraux,* III, 180.

66. *Ibid.*, p. 149.

67. *Ibid.*, I, 198.

68. Lalourcé and Duval, eds., *Cahiers,* IV, articles 105, 161–63 of the nobility's cahier.

69. *Ibid.*, I, 199, 211.

70. Noël Valois, *Inventaire des arrêts du conseil d'état* (1886), introduction.

71. *Inventaire sommaire des Archives Départementales antérieures à 1790: Haute-Garonne,* Sér. C, t. II (Toulouse, 1903), p. 152. Other schools established by the nobility were at La Rochelle, Pont-à-Mousson, Nevers, and Saumur. Elizabeth S. Teall, "The Public Mind of the

Noblesse d'Epée, 1484–1589," (unpubl. dissertation, Radcliffe, 1959), p. 452.

72. The best analysis of the edict of La Paulette and its implications is by Roland Mousnier, *La vénalité des offices* (Rouen, n.d.).

73. Anon., *Remonstrance faicte par deux cents gentilshommes français au chancelier* (n.p., 1615), p. 7.

74. Richelieu, *Maximes d'état ou testament politique*, p. 223.

75. Anon., *A monseigneur l'illustrissime et eminentissime cardinal, duc et pair de France* ... (Paris, 1634), pp. 5, 8–9, 11.

NOTES TO CHAPTER 4

1. Octave Le Maire, *L'Imprescriptibilité de l'ancienne noblesse et la dérogeance d'après la jurisprudence ancienne* (Bruxelles, 1953), pp. 19–20.

2. *Ibid.*

3. Académie des sciences morales et politiques, *Catalogue des actes de François Ier*, IV (1890), 98; VII (1896), 447. Paris.

4. Tiraqueau, *Tractatus de nobilitate* (Paris, 1549), pp. 181–83.

5. Estienne Pasquier, *Recherches de la France*, livre II, ch. xvii, in *Oeuvres*, I, 134.

6. Paul Viollet, *Histoire du droit civil français* (Paris, 1905), p. 280; François Olivier-Martin, *Histoire de la coutume de Paris* (Paris, 1922–30), I, 125; Henri Carré, *La noblesse de France et l'opinion publique au XVIIIe siècle* (Paris, 1920), p. 136.

7. Gaston Zeller, "Louis XI, la noblesse, et la marchandise," *Annales: Economies, sociétés, civilisations*, I (1946), 333–36.

8. The ordinances of 1560 and 1579 are in Isambert, *Recueil général des anciennes lois françaises*, XIV, 91, 394.

9. *Le paysan françois*, p. 142. This anonymous work, written about 1614, did not express a simple class point of view, but it did show some understanding of the nobility's problems.

10. L.N.H. Chérin, *La noblesse considérée sous ses divers rapports* (Paris, 1788), pp. 92–93. Cf. the Abbé Coyer's statement, in 1756, that the demand to engage in commerce came from the obscure country nobility who were "helplessly watching the châteaux of their fathers crumble in ruins." *La noblesse commerçante* (London, 1756), p. 9.

11. Gaston Rambert, ed., *Histoire du commerce de Marseille* (Paris, 1949–57), III, 208–9.

12. Chérin, *La noblesse*, pp. 218, 283.

13. The works of Laffemas are listed in J. J. Champollion-Figeac, ed., *Documents historiques inédits tirés des collections manuscrites de la Bibliothèque Nationale*, IV (Paris, 1848), p. viii.

14. Barthélemy de Laffemas, *Le plaisir de la noblesse et autres qui ont des éritages aux champs* (Paris, 1603).

15. G. Fagniez, *L'Economie sociale de la France sous Henri IV* (Paris, 1897), p. 90.

16. Permezel, *La politique financiére de Sully dans la généralité de Lyon* (Lyon, 1935), p. 47.

17. Fagniez, *L'Economie sociale*, p. 252.

18. As quoted in Emile Levasseur, *Histoire du commerce de la France* (Paris, 1911), I, 259.

19. Laurent Bouchel, *La bibliothèque ou thrésor du droit françois* (Paris, 1615), I, 142.

20. Claude de Bonnault, "La société française au XVIe siècle, 1515–1614," *Bull. Rech. Hist.*, LXII (1956), 85.

21. "Il y en a qui disent que c'est un Art necessaire, que les Marchans sont amis du peuple, le secours des pauvres: la commodité des riches: que plusieurs Roys, Princes, & Grand Personnages s'en sont meslez." Thierriat, *Trois traités de la noblesse de race, de la noblesse civile & des immunitez des ignobles*, p. 113.

22. Antoyne de Montchrétien, *Traicté de l'oeconomie politique*, ed. Théodore Funck-Brentano (Paris, 1889), pp. 22, 30, 32–33, 40, 43, 48–49, 59, 65, 139, 353, 356.

23. Chérin, *La noblesse*, p. 283.

24. As quoted in C. W. Cole, *French Mercantilist Doctrines Before Colbert* (New York, 1931), p. 204.

25. Isambert, *Recueil général*, XVI, 339.

26. *Ibid.*

27. The Thracians, Scythians, Persians, Egyptians, Lydians, Lacedaemonians, Athenians, Thebans, and Romans were all believed to have expelled from the nobility anyone who engaged in commerce. Estienne Pasquier, in *Oeuvres*, I, 134; Du Rivault, *Les états, esquels il est discouru du prince, du noble, et du tiers estat*, pp. 221–23; Le Bret, *Oeuvres*, pp. 531–34; Thierriat, *Trois traités*, p. 112; Bouchel, *La bibliothèque*, II, 274; Boyssat, *Remerciement au roy par les annoblis du Dauphiné où il est touché de la dignité de la noblesse*, p. 7.

Tiraqueau traced the origins of dérogeance back to Noah and Adam; Gilles-André La Roque saw its beginning in heaven. La Bigne de Villeneuve, *Essai sur la théorie de dérogeance*, p. 69.

28. Le Maire, *L'Imprescriptibilité*, p. 59.

29. Du Rivault, *Les états*, pp. 221–22.

30. Thierriat, *Trois traités*, pp. 114, 129.

31. Chérin, *La noblesse*, pp. 104, 155–56, 250.

32. *Catalogue des actes de François Ier*, VII, 447.

33. *Le paysan françois*, p. 142.

34. Loyseau, *Traité des ordres et simples dignitez*, ch. v, para. 101, 102, 106, 108, in *Oeuvres*.

35. The ordinance of 1560, for instance, excluded from trade both nobles and officeholders. Isambert, *Recueil général*, XIV, 91. See also Thierriat, *Trois traités*, pp. 339–41. It will be recalled that some local magistrates as well as judges on the Parlements and other courts enjoyed tax exemptions.

36. L'Alouëte, *Des affaires d'estat, des finances, du prince et de sa noblesse*, p. 185; Thierriat, *Trois traités*, pp. 82–83; Le Maire, *L'imprescriptibilité*, pp. 23–25, 61–62.

37. Guillaume d'Oncieu, *La précédence de la noblesse sus un différent en cas de précédence* (Lyon, 1593), pp. 43–46.

38. La Noue, *Discours politiques et militaires*, pp. 204–9. Other examples, among many, of the praise of aristocratic estate life are in Du Fail, *Contes et discours d'Eutrapel*, II, 38.

39. Oncieu, *La précédence*, pp. 43–50.

40. Thierriat, *Trois traités*, pp. 80–81.

41. Du Rivault, *Les états*, pp. 221–23. See also Le Bret, *Oeuvres*, pp. 532ff.

42. *Le paysan françois*, pp. 140–42.

43. Glass is the product of a science so noble, and gives such pleasure, it was argued, that glassmaking could hardly be regarded as demeaning. Le Bret, *Oeuvres*, pp. 532ff.

44. Rambert, ed., *Histoire*, III, 208–9; Permezel, *La politique*, p. 47.

45. *Le paysan françois*, p. 144; Pierre Jacques Brillon, *Dictionnaire des arrêts ou jurisprudence universelle des parlemens de France*, rev. ed. (Paris, 1727), IV, 484; Le Maire, *L'Imprescriptibilité*, pp. 29–30; Le Bret, *Oeuvres*, p. 534; and Imbart de La Tour, *Les origines de la Réforme*, I, 397–400.

46. Warren C. Scoville, "The French Economy in 1700–1701: An Appraisal by the Deputies of Trade," *Journal of Economic History*, XXII (1962), 246.

47. The importance of the nobility's traditional attitude to the general "anti-capitalistic" atmosphere of modern France is explored by David S. Landes, "French Entrepreneurship and Industrial Growth in the Nineteenth Century," *Journal of Economic History*, IX (1949), 54–55.

48. Montesquieu, *The Spirit of the Laws*, tr. Thomas Nugent (New York, 1949), I, 327.

NOTES TO CHAPTER 5

1. See, for instance, François Ragueau's repetition of the old platitudes, from Aristotle, Cicero, and others. *Indice des droits roiaux et*

seigneuriaux, rev. ed. (Paris, 1600), pp. 387–88. On the Italian background, see Aldo Vallone, *Cortesia e nobilità nel Rinascimento* (Asti, 1955), p. 50; Jacob Burckhardt, *The Civilization of the Renaissance in Italy* (New York, 1954), pp. 265–72; and G. M. Vogt, "Gleanings for the History of a Sentiment: *Generositas virtus, non sanguis,*" in *Journal of English and Germanic Philology,* XXIV (1925), 102–24.

2. La Perrière, *Le miroir politique, contenant diverses manières de gouverner et policer les republiques,* p. 110.

3. Estienne Pasquier, *Oeuvres,* I, 135.

4. Louis Ernaud, *Discours de la noblesse et des justes moyens d'y parvenir* (Caen, 1584), preface.

5. Tiraqueau, *Tractatus de nobilitate,* ch. 24; Froydeville, *Dialogues de l'origine de la noblesse,* pp. 24–25, 61–62, 74, 77, 87; L'Alouëte, *Des affaires d'estat, des finances, du prince et de sa noblesse,* pp. 144–47.

6. Nicolas Pasquier, *Le gentilhomme* (Paris, 1611), pp. 1–2.

7. François Olivier-Martin, "Noël du Fail et le rôle social de la noblesse," *Mém. de la soc. d'hist. et d'arch. de Bretagne,* VIII (1927), 274–75.

8. Regnier de La Planche, *Histoire de l'estat de France* (Paris, 1836), p. 302. First ed. 1576.

9. Louis Musset, *Discours sur les remontrances & reformation de chacun état* (Paris, 1582), p. 164.

10. Olivier-Martin, in *Mém. de la soc. d'hist. et d'arch. de Bretagne,* VIII (1927), 269.

11. Jherome des Osres, *Les deux livres de la noblesse civile* (Paris, 1549), p. 19.

12. L'Alouëte, *Affaires,* p. 184. Cf. Ernaud, *Discours,* pp. 25–27, on "le bon natural" of nobles.

13. Du Rivault, *Les états, esquels il est discouru du prince, du noble, et du tiers estat,* pp. 270–73.

14. Nicolas Pasquier, *Le gentilhomme,* pp. 2–3, 10–12.

15. La Perrière, *Le miroir politique,* p. 112.

16. Froydeville, *Dialogues,* p. 41.

17. Ernaud, *Discours,* p. 4.

18. Du Rivault, *Les états,* p. 274. Cf. Jean-Baptiste Nenna, *Traicté de la noblesse* (Paris, 1583), pp. 102f.

19. Thierriat, *Trois traités; de la noblesse de race, de la noblesse civile & des immunitez des ignobles,* pp. 80–81.

20. Loyseau, *Ordres,* ch. IV, para. 1–3, in *Oeuvres.*

21. "Outre les communes instructions [la maison] est enrichie de mille petits esguillons d'honneur, dont les enfans nobles ont leurs tendres aureilles tellement battues." Du Rivault, *Les états,* p. 275.

22. For a brief outline of Nenna's work and its place in the Italian

courtesy tradition, see James W. Holme, "Italian Courtesy-Books of the Sixteenth Century," *The Modern Language Review*, V (1910), 153–56.

23. Nenna, *Traicté de la noblesse*, p. 156.

24. Froydeville, *Dialogues*, p. 38.

25. *Ibid.*, pp. 61–62.

26. L'Alouëte, *Affaires*, p. 213. The section on nobility is basically unchanged from the earlier *Traité des nobles*.

27. *Ibid.*

28. *Ibid.*, pp. 213–14.

29. Ernaud, *Discours*, pp. 24, 27ff, 40–41.

30. Du Rivault, *Les états*, pp. 360–61.

31. *Ibid.*, pp. 270–77.

32. *Ibid.*, pp. 329–30.

33. Thierriat, *Trois traités*, p. 145.

34. *Ibid.*, pp. 143–44, 160.

35. Montaigne, *Essays*, tr. E. J. Trechmann, III, 5.

36. Oncieu, *La précédence de la noblesse sus un différent en cas de précédence*, pp. 10–11.

37. Froydeville, *Dialogues*, pp. 72–73.

38. L'Alouëte, *Affaires*, pp. 211–12.

39. "Jamais heretique ne fut noble: ils sont tous menteurs, tous vilains, tous lasches, & de coeur failly. Le Catholique est vraiment noble." Jean de Caumont, *De la vertu de noblesse* (Paris, 1585), p. 5.

40. Des Osres, *Les deux livres*, pp. 20, 58–59.

41. Pierre Charron, *De la sagesse* (Lyon, 1606), pp. 275–79.

42. See, for instance, Raymond L. Kilgour, "Brantôme's Account of Sixteenth-Century Chivalry," *Harvard Studies & Notes in Philology and Literature*, XIX (1937), 131, 133–34.

43. Du Rivault, *Les états*, p. 213.

44. Brillon, *Dictionnaire des arrêts ou jurisprudence universelle*, rev. ed., IV, 483.

45. Caumont, *De la vertu de noblesse*, p. 10.

46. Thierriat, *Trois traités*, pp. 143ff.

47. Oncieu, *La précédence*, pp. 10–11.

48. *Ibid.*, p. 42.

49. *Ibid.*, p. 12.

NOTES TO CHAPTER 6

1. "The nobility is now so bastardized that all of the orders are overturned and perverted, and often the last run to the rank of the first without any respect or honor for antiquity." L'Alouëte, *Des affaires*

d'estat, des finances, du prince et de sa noblesse, p. 189. La Noue made the same charge. *Discours politiques et militaires,* p. 108.

2. Jacques Leschassier, *La maladie de la France, presenté l'an 1602 au Roy,* in *Oeuvres* (Paris, 1652), pp. 215-16. See Du Fail's description (a portion of which is at the head of this chapter) of the social structure as "un désordre." *Les contes et discours d'Eutrapel,* I, 67. "Confusion has entered," said Pierre d'Origny, *Le hérault de la noblesse de France* (Reims, 1578), p. 30. The Burgundy Estates complained in 1587 of confusion among the three estates. Georges Weill, *Les états de Bourgogne sous Henri III,* in *Mém. Soc. bourguignonne de géog. et d'hist.,* IX (1893), 133. If the intermingling of classes continues, said another, "all will be confused." Thierriat, *Trois traités; de la noblesse de race, de la noblesse civile & des immunitez des ignobles,* pp. 299-300.

3. Such intermarriage was described as "the means of maintaining oneself in property by marrying women of lesser rank but greater property, which is the main profit and support of the nobility." Leschassier, in *Oeuvres,* p. 217.

4. L'Alouëte, *Affaires,* pp. 226-29; Louis Le Caron, *Pandectes ou digestes du droict françois,* rev. ed. (Paris, 1637), p. 73.

5. L'Alouëte, *Affaires,* pp. 226-29. It was true that the children were not guilty, L'Alouëte admitted, but they had to suffer the consequences of their fathers' sins, in order to discourage men from "this vile sin."

6. Brillon, *Dictionnaire des arrêts ou jurisprudence universelle des parlemens de France,* rev. ed., I, 541.

7. Yvonne Bézard, *La vie rurale dans le sud de la région parisienne, 1450-1560* (Paris, 1929), pp. 68-69, 75-79; Paul Raveau, *Essai sur la situation économique et l'état social en Poitou au XVIe siècle* (Paris, 1931); Giuliano Procacci, *Classi sociali e monarchia assoluta nella Francia della prima metà del secolo XVI* (Turin, 1955); E. LeRoy Ladurie, "Sur Montpellier et sa campagne aux XVIe et XVIIe siècles," *Annales E.S.C.,* XII (1957), 223-30. The well-known sale of the Constable Bourbon's estates—37 out of 40 seigneuries going to roturiers—is recounted by Romier, *Le royaume de Catherine de Médicis,* I, 184.

8. Bézard, *La vie rurale,* p. 79.

9. A good description of the process is given by J.-R. Bloch, *L'Anoblissement en France au temps de François Ier* (Paris, 1934), pp. 54-55. The following contemporary description of "usurpation" would seem to indicate, however, that possession of an estate could come late, after one had already been seeking to become identified as a noble. "Several were able to become gentlemen, or acquire the reputation of being such, by living in the noble style (which some misinterpreted as meaning to live from one's rents without doing anything), abstaining from

mechanical work, carrying a sword at the side, wearing clothing appropriate to the class, establishing alliances with nobles, and making some slight profession of arms. Then afterwards if some little noble fief or some position of authority fell into their hands, they were forthwith labeled noble lords or at least honorable squires." Ernaud, *Discours de la noblesse et des justes moyens d'y parvenir*, pp. 11–12.

10. Crest, *Le cabinet du roy de France, dans lequel il y a trois perles precieuses*, p. 294.

11. For complaints and recriminations against the usurpers, see Chérin, *La noblesse considérée sous ses divers rapports*, pp. 42–43, 52–53, 61–62, 90, 105–6, 137–38, 166, 176–77, 219, 230–31. Many anti-usurpation ordinances are conveniently assembled in Chérin, *Abrégé chronologique*, pp. 871, 872–73, 877–88, 890–91, 897–99, 908–11. Arrêts forbidding usurpation were issued by the Parlement of Paris in 1555, 1560, 1576, 1577, 1579, 1582, and 1600. Pierre Guénois, *La grande conférence des ordonnances* (n.p., 1678), II, 1164; III, 386.

12. Bloch, *L'Anoblissement*, p. 191.

13. Gilles-André La Roque, "Mémoire sur la recherche de la noblesse," p. 7, in *Traité de la noblesse* (Rouen, 1734).

14. Pierre Lebeurier, *État des anoblis en Normandie, 1545–1661* (Evreux, 1866), p. xix. See also Renée Taffan de Kymadec, "Les lettres d'anoblissement sos les règnes de Henri IV et Louis XIII" (unpubl. thesis, Paris, 1954), where 527 ennoblements are listed for the reign of Henry IV and 372 for that of Louis XIII; these figures are conservative, since some of the records are no longer extant.

15. For samples of the standard letters of ennoblement, see Thierriat, *Trois traités*, pp. 168–71. An analytical study of the forms of ennoblement under Francis I can be found in Bloch, *L'Anoblissement*, pp. 133–40.

16. Of the coutumiers edited or revised during the late sixteenth century, two or three, like the custom of Laon, published in the late 1550's, included the anoblis in their definition of "noblesse." Others mentioned the nobility but said nothing to indicate that anoblis were included or excluded. Charles A. Bourdot de Richebourg, *Nouveau coutumier général* (Paris, 1724), II, 414, 444, 820, 872, 669, 683; III, 240, 351, 353, 381.

17. See, for example, Le Caron, *Pandectes*, p. 73.

18. Du Fail, *Contes et discours d'Eutrapel*, II, 161.

19. Le Bret, *Oeuvres*, p. 64; Thierriat, *Trois traités*, p. 204.

20. Brillon, *Dictionnaire*, I, 202. Brillon's conclusion, based on a case of 1577, was that ennoblement of the father by royal letters patent extended to children born prior to the ennoblement.

21. Thierriat, *Trois traités*, pp. 166, 211–16, 227, 250–54.

22. For a convenient introduction to the municipal nobility, see Bloch, *L'Anoblissement*, pp. 102–23.

23. See the older and not entirely satisfactory study of J. Trévédy, *Sur le titre de "Noble homme"* (Vannes, 1902); cf. Bloch, p. 119.

24. G. Tholin, "Des tailles et des impositions au pays d'Agenais durant le XVIᵉ siècle," *Recueil des travaux de la Soc. d'agric., sciences et arts d'Agen*, 2d series, IV (1875), 91–135; Eustache Piémond, *Mémoires ... 1572–1608* (Valence, 1885), p. 356.

25. The Cour des Aides did not finally "arrive" until 1645; the Chambre des Comptes of Dijon, in 1650; of Brittany, in 1659; of Dauphiny, in 1650; of Nantes, in 1692. Brillon, *Dictionnaire*, I, 406.

26. I do not know how far back the expression *noblesse de robe* can be traced. *Gens de robe* was very old, as was the distinction between *robe longue* and *robe courte*. By our period, certainly, these were sometimes referred to as nobles, as in the phrase "nobles de longue et courte robe." *Cayer presenté au roy par ceux du tiers estat de Dauphiné* (Grenoble, 1619). First ed., 1603.

27. Guy Pape, Quest. 88, 389, as cited in Brillon, *Dictionnaire*, I, 354; Joseph Dubreuil, *Analyse raisonée de la legislation sur les eaux* (Aix, 1842).

28. Bouchel, *La bibliothèque ou thrésor du droit françois*, I, 134.

29. Dubreuil, *Analyse*, pp. 28–29.

30. *Ibid.*, pp. 27–42.

31. Crest, *Le cabinet*, p. 295. For additional contemporary uses of the term "new nobles" or "new nobility," see Le Caron, *Pandectes*, p. 176; Ernaud, *Discours*, p. 13; L'Alouëte, *Traité des nobles et des vertus dont ils sont formez*, p. 65; Du Rivault, *Les états, esquels il est discouru du prince, du noble, et du tiers-état*, pp. 293–94.

32. Chérin, *Abrégé chronologique*, pp. 850–52, cites an estimate based on the large-scale program to list nobles in 1660.

33. Du Fail, *Contes et discours*, I, 67. Du Fail was referring particularly to Brittany.

34. Origny, *Le hérault*, p. 30.

35. Chérin, *La noblesse*, p. 166.

36. Montand, *Le miroir des françois*, p. 234; Origny, *Le hérault*, p. 30, 41; anon., *Anatomie des trois ordres de la France, sur le sujet des estats* (1615), pp. 22–23.

37. F. Grimaudet, *Remonstrances aux estatz d'Anjou* (Paris, 1560), as cited in Romier, *Le royaume de Catherine de Médicis*, I, 186. Romier feels that the new nobility was created for the most part by legal procedures, but in view of the relatively small number of ennoblements, particularly before 1560, and of the complaints about large numbers of false nobles, I find this hard to believe.

38. Douais, ed., *Mémoires sur l'état du clergé, de la noblesse, de la justice et du peuple dans les diocèses de Narbonne, de Montpellier et de Castres en 1573*, p. 41.

39. Anon., *Responce à une lettre envoyée par un gentilhomme de basse Bretagne à un sien amy estant à la suitte de la cour sur le misere de ce temps* (Rouen, n.d.).

40. "Or si la Noblesse neuve n'est tant à priser que ceste ancienne de laquelle nous avons ja parlé, elle n'est pourtant à mépriser puisque c'est toujours Noblesse." Du Rivault, *Les etats*, pp. 293–94.

41. Leschassier, in *Oeuvres*, pp. 215–16; cf. p. 9, above.

42. L'Hospital's statement is in Mayer, ed., *Des états généraux et autres assemblées nationales* (Paris, 1789), X, 325–335; Henri Sée, *Les états de Bretagne au XV*[e] *siècle* (Paris, 1895), p. 16.

43. La Noue, *Discours*, pp. 38, 66; Lalourcé and Duval, eds., *Cahiers*, I, 237; II, 190; III, 137, 145–46.

44. For contemporary listings of the noble privileges, see Tiraqueau, *Tractatus de nobilitate*, ch. 20; and Thierriat, *Trois traités*, pp. 32–74. Both Zeller and Doucet, *Les institutions de la France au XVI*[e] *siècle* (Paris, 1948) contain modern summaries.

45. Chérin, *Abrégé chronologique*, pp. 871, 872–77, 894–95; Isambert, XIV, 108, 159, 178, 260, 305, 327, 538; XV, 90. The dates of these vestimentary decrees were 1543, 1547, 1549, 1561, 1563, 1565, 1567, 1573, 1576, 1577, 1583, 1594, and 1615.

46. Chérin, *La noblesse*, pp. 53–54; La Noue, pp. 15, 32, 93, 96, 157ff; Lalourcé et Duval, *Cahiers*, I, 210, 235, 237; II, 190; III, 137, 145–46.

47. Lalourcé and Duval, *Cahiers*, I, 237; II, 190; III, 137, 145–46.

48. Du Fail, *Contes et discours*, I, 66–67.

49. As quoted in Henri Noëll, *Henri II et la naissance de la société moderne* (Paris, 1944), p. 302.

50. Thierriat, *Trois traités*, p. 70.

51. Anon., *Advis au roy . . . des moyens de bannir le luxe du royaume, d'establir un grand nombre de manufactures en iceluy* (1614), p. 13.

52. The La Mothe case of February 1546, for example, led to a decision that with respect to intestate succession a councillor of the Parlement of Paris would be treated as a noble. (Le Caron, *Pandectes*, p. 72.) In 1573, in the famous Jacques Mesnager case, it was stated more generally that the inheritance of all councillors of the Parlement of Paris would be divided according to the rules of noble succession. For other legal cases see Jean Bacquet, *Oeuvres* (Paris, 1621), ch. 19; Thierriat, *Trois traités*, p. 186; Le Bret, *Oeuvres*, pp. 525–27; Brillon, *Dictionnaire*, I, 202; IV, 498; Loyseau, *Offices*, liv. I, ch. 9.

53. The arrêt of 1593 indicated that one must prove that his father

and grandfather had "lived in the noble manner" in order to claim "nobility of blood." Brillon, *Dictionnaire*, IV, 498.

54. *Ibid.*, I, 202.

55. Le Bret, *Oeuvres*, pp. 525–27.

56. L'Alouëte's original work was entitled *Traité des nobles et des vertus dont ils sont formez* (Paris, 1577). It was reprinted as part of *Des affaires d'estat, des finances, du prince et de sa noblesse* (Metz, 1597). See pp. 186–204 for L'Alouëte's analysis and his recommendations.

57. Isambert, *Recueil général des anciennes lois françaises*, XV, 234. Article 26.

58. Ibid., Article 25.

59. Le Bret, *Oeuvres*, p. 63.

60. Ragueau, *Indice des droits roiaux et seigneuriaux*, p. 389.

61. Bacquet, *Oeuvres*, pp. 3, 66, 69–72.

62. Thierriat, *Trois traités*. In speaking of nobles, Thierriat used the first person plural. Pp. 47–48.

63. Loyseau later complained that Thierriat had merely translated and abridged Tiraqueau's work, but that put it too strongly. Loyseau, *Ordres*, V.69.

64. Thierriat, *Trois traités*, pp. 331–32.

65. *Ibid.*, pp. 145, 157–60, 250–54.

66. *Ibid.*, pp. 143–44.

67. "Il y a des degrez entre les gentils-hommes, & de la preference des uns aux autres. Les uns sont superieurs, les autres inferieurs: les uns de toutes parts nobles, les autres d'une part seulement, ou de quelques parts & non de toutes." *Ibid.*, pp. 10–11.

68. *Ibid.*, pp. 39–40, 166, 211–16, 227, 250–54.

69. *Ibid.*, pp. 11–16.

70. *Ibid.*, pp. 16–19.

71. *Ibid.*, p. 44.

72. *Cinq livres des droits des offices* (Paris, 1610) and *Traité des ordres et simples dignitez* (Paris, 1613) have been brought together, along with other works, in Loyseau, *Oeuvres* (various editions). I have used the edition of 1640. The references are to chapter and paragraph.

73. Loyseau, *Ordres*, V.61–63.

74. *Ibid.*, IV.34; V.34–38.

75. *Ibid.*, V.51–60.

76. *Ibid.*, V.60.

77. "Ces ennoblissemens purgent le sang & posterité de l'ennobli de toute tache de roture, & le reduisent en mesme qualité & dignité, que

si de tout temps sa race eust esté ingenuë. . . . Toutefois pource que *indulgentia illa quos liberat notat* [Loyseau's italics] & qu'à bien entendre, cette abolition de servitude ou de roture, n'est qu'un effaceure, dont la marque demeure, voire semble plustost un fiction qu'une vérité . . . de là vient, qu'en l'opinion des hommes, on n'estime pas tant les ennoblis, soit par lettres ou par dignitez, que les Nobles de race." *Ibid.,* IV.42–43.

78. Loyseau, *Offices,* IX.46, 47.

79. *Ibid.,* VII.64.

80. *Ibid.,* IX.19–21.

81. *Ibid.,* IX.27, 32–33.

82. *Ibid.,* IX.18.

83. Ce qui merite bien d'estre expliqué à loisir, pour ce qu'aucuns en veulent douter." *Ibid.,* IX.5.

84. *Anon., Discours d'un gentilhomme françois à la noblesse de France, sur l'ouverture de l'assemblée des états généraux dans la ville de Paris en ceste année 1614* (n.p., n.d.).

85. *Ibid.,* pp. 8–9.

86. *Ibid.,* p. 54.

87. *Ibid.,* pp. 23–24.

88. *Ibid.,* pp. 21–22.

89. *Ibid.,* p. 59.

90. *Ibid.,* pp. 56–57.

91. *Ibid.,* p. 57.

92. *Ibid.,* p. 60.

93. *Ibid.,* p. 62.

94. *Ibid.,* pp. 59–62.

95. L'Alouëte, *Traité des nobles,* p. 65.

96. Du Fail, *Contes et discours,* II, 41.

97. Loyseau, *Ordres,* V.20, in *Oeuvres.*

98. Anon., *Le paysan françois,* pp. 21–22.

99. Nathan Edelman, *Attitudes of Seventeenth Century France Toward the Middle Ages* (New York, 1946), p. 51n.

100. "Plusieurs gens de Justice & de robe longue, commencerent à prendre dedans leurs familles cette qualité de Nobles. . . . Mais aussi par la voix commune du peuple cette Noblesse fut estimée comme bastards. Parce que tels personnages ne font profession des armes." Estienne Pasquier, *Oeuvres* (Amsterdam, 1723), I, 135.

101. Down to 1604, at the very least, the available marriage records show that the families of robe were still "neatly separated from the nobility." Mousnier, *La vénalité des offices sous Henri IV et Louis XIII* (Rouen, n.d.), p. 507.

1. Most of the writers mentioned in this chapter can be found in at least one of the following sources: *Dictionnaire de biographie française* (Paris, 1933–   ); *Dictionnaire des lettres françaises: Le seizième. siècle* (Paris, 1951); *La grande encyclopédie* (Paris, 1886–1902); Louis Moreri, ed., *Le grand dictionnaire historique* (Paris, 1579). For many of them there are longer studies, even complete biographies, which supply much more detail. E. and E. Haag, *La France Protestante* (Paris, 1858–88) provides information on the religious affiliations of a number of writers discussed here.

2. Montaigne's description of a "quatriesme estat," the noblesse de robe, is applicable, at least in part, to himself. *Essays* (tr. Trechmann), Bk. I, ch. 23.

Glossary

Anobli. A person who had been officially granted noble status by means of royal letters patent. His children and grandchildren were also considered anoblis. The passage of time was supposed to make anoblis full-fledged nobles, but social acceptance did not always correspond to legal status.

Arrêt. A decree or judgment, usually by one of the Parlements or other sovereign courts.

Avocat. A lawyer or attorney, or, according to English practice, a barrister.

Bailli. Traditionally the chief administrative and judicial officer on the regional or local level. Almost always from the old nobility. The baillis' power diminished during the sixteenth century, as judicial functions were turned over to lieutenants trained in the law, and royal treasurers were assigned to each province to supervise tax collecting. Nevertheless, they retained some importance. One of their specific responsibilities was supervision of the *ban et arrière-ban* in their districts.

Bailliage. Territorial jurisdiction of a *bailli*; roughly a bailiwick or county. At the beginning of the sixteenth century there were 86 bailliages in France.

Ban et arrière-ban. Traditionally the military service owed to the king by his vassals and rear-vassals. By the sixteenth century this service was the obligation of all who held "noble" lands, but in practice many paid a fee in lieu of actual service and others were officially exempt. The ban et arrière-ban was called up infrequently— only four times by Charles IX, twice by Henry III, and twice by Henry IV.

Compagnies d'ordonnance. Ordnance companies; heavy cavalry. See also *gendarme.*

Corvée. Labor service owed to a seigneur by his peasant tenants, usually one to three days a year. By the turn of the sixteenth century, most of these labor obligations had been abandoned or replaced by a monetary payment, but there were still some efforts to enforce or revive the corvée.

Coutumier. A written statement of the customary law and usages of a given province or locality. There was an extensive program of codification and publication of coutumiers during the sixteenth century.

Franc-fief. A payment to the king by *roturiers* holding fiefs or noble lands. When this payment was called for, at intervals of twenty or thirty years, investigations were conducted to determine who was required to pay. These investigations should have provided official indications of class status, but numerous exemptions from payment granted to the inhabitants of certain towns and lax enforcement made the distinctions ambiguous.

Gendarme. A heavy cavalryman belonging to one of the *compagnies d'ordonnance* created during the closing phase of the Hundred Years' War. Each company was comprised of a certain number of "lances"—originally one hundred but eventually as few as twenty-five or thirty. Each lance included one gendarme (or *homme d'armes*) and from three to five valets and archers. The gendarme was the leader. Gendarmes were supposed to be nobles, but many exceptions were made.

Grands-Jours. Special commissions designated by one of the Parlements to hold court sessions in a specified location. Members of the Parlement were named to this commission, which had both civil and criminal jurisdiction. Somewhat comparable to assizes, the Grands-Jours were held intermittently, usually in provinces distant from a Parlement, where disorder had run rampant.

Métayer. A farmer who paid rent in kind, the landowner furnishing stock and seed. A sharecropper. Regional variations existed, but usually the métayer received one half of the production after deducting the cost of stock, seed, and harvest.

Noblesse civile. One of the theoretical subdivisions of the noble class. Those entitled to noble status by virtue of administrative or governmental service.

Noblesse de cloche. Magistrates, or holders of municipal office, whose positions were considered sufficiently honorable and prestigious to raise them to the new nobility.

Noblesse d'épée. The nobility of the sword. Roughly synonymous with the "old" nobility.

Noblesse de mérites. A theoretical noble status based on individual merit; usually contrasted to noble status that was inherited or purchased.

Noblesse de race. Noble status attained by being born into a noble family. Usually contrasted with the "new nobility"; roughly comparable to the *noblesse d'épée* or the "old nobility."

Noblesse de robe. Category of the nobility that owed its status to judicial offices, especially in the Parlements. A subdivision of the "new nobility" along with *anoblis* and *noblesse de cloche*; there was considerable overlapping of these ranks.

Plaidoyer. Address before a court of law, especially the plea of counsel for the defense.

Roturier. Commoner. In France all those not of the clergy or nobility were considered roturiers. The collective or abstract noun, referring to the commonality or to common status, is *roture*.

Taillable. A person subject to payment of the taille; not exempt.

Taille. The most basic direct tax of France from the Middle Ages to the Revolution. It has been called a tax of "repartition": the total amount to be raised was decided upon by the central government; quotas were then assigned to the different provinces, bailliages, and finally each village or parish. Amounts collected from individuals were then determined on the basis of such factors as land holdings, previous contributions, and declared income, but procedures varied from region to region. Regional inequities, poor records, and collection machinery that encouraged maximum demands discredited the taille. Its most serious weakness was the fact that those best able to contribute were exempt. In addition to the inhabitants of privileged towns, holders of specified offices, and many individual bourgeois, the clergy and the nobility as a whole were exempt from payment of the taille.

Taille réelle. A method of collecting the *taille* in certain provinces. Landed estates were designated as either noble (those which had once been fiefs or estates of the old noble families) or common (all the rest). The taille was then assessed on the common or roturier estates, regardless of the personal status of the owner.

Taille personelle. A method of collecting the *taille* based on personal status. Nobles were exempt. Most of France followed this procedure.

Sénéchal. Term used in southern France to designate a *bailli*. The jurisdiction of the sénéchal, equivalent to a *bailliage*, was a *sénéchausée*.

Bibliographical Materials

SELECTED PRIMARY SOURCES

Abregé des escritures fournies de la part de la noblesse du Dauphiné contre le tiers estat dudit pais. N.p., n.d.

Advertissement envoyé à la noblesse de France, tant du parti du roy, que des rebelles & coniurez. Paris, 1574.

Advis au roy ... des moyens de bannir le luxe du royaume, d'establir un grand nombre de manufactures en iceluy. N.p., 1614.

Advis, remonstrances et requestes aux estats généraux tenus à Paris, 1614. Par six paysans.

A monseigneur l'illustrissime et eminentissime cardinal, duc et pair de France sur la déclaration du roy, publiée en faveur de sa noblesse et à la descharge de ses subjets. Paris, 1634.

Anatomie des trois ordres de la France, sur le sujet des estats. N.p., 1615.

Angot de l'Eperonnière, Robert. Oeuvres satyriques. Ed. Fr. Lachèvre. Paris, 1929. First ed., 1617.

Avis au roi pour faire entrer la noblesse et gens de mérite aux charges, & pourvoir au prix excessif des offices, sans mescontenter les officiers. Paris, 1617. First ed., 1615.

Bacquet, Jean. Oeuvres. Paris, 1621.

Bengi-Puyvallée, Maurice de. "Extraits des cahiers des assemblées du tiers état du duché de Berry en 1576 et 1588," Mém. de la société des antiquaires du Centre. Vols. XLVII–XLVIII (1934–35).

Bernard, Auguste, ed. Procés-verbaux des états-généraux de 1593. Paris, 1842.

Béroalde de Verville, François. Dialogue de la vertu. Paris, 1584.

———. Le moyen de parvenir. Ed. Paul Lacroix. Paris, 1840. This may be the edition described by Brunet as published 1841, ed. Paul L. [Lacroix] Jacob, bibliophile.

Bodin, Jean. Oeuvres philosophiques. Ed. P. Mesnard. Paris, 1951.

———. Les six livres de la république. Paris, 1576.

Bouchel, Laurent. La bibliothèque ou thrésor du droit françois. 2 vols. Paris, 1615.

Boyssat, Pierre de. Remerciement au roy par les annoblis du Dauphiné, où il est touché de la dignité de la noblesse. Paris, 1603.

Brantôme, Pierre de Bourdeilles, Seigneur de. Oeuvres complètes. Ed. Lalanne. 13 vols. Paris, 1858–95.

Brillon, Pierre Jacques. Dictionnaire des arrêts ou jurisprudence universelle des parlemens de France. 6 vols. Rev. ed. Paris, 1727.

Brosse, Claude. Cayer presenté au roy, par le sieur Claude Brosse. Grenoble, 1621.

"Cahier de la noblesse de Languedoc, 1614," in Dom Vaissette, Histoire générale de Languedoc, XII, 1638–48. Toulouse, 1890.

Cajetan, Cardinal [Cajetano, Cardinal Enrico]. Lettres de monseigneur le cardinal Caietan … envoyées à la noblesse de France. Lyon, 1590.

Catalogue des actes de François Ier. Ed. Paul Marichal. 10 vols. Paris, 1888–1908.

Caumont, Jean de. De la vertu de noblesse. Paris, 1585.

Cayer presenté au roy par ceux du tiers estat de Dauphiné. Grenoble, 1619.

Champollion-Figeac, Jean-Jacques, ed. Documents historiques inédits tirés des collections manuscrites de la Bibliothèque Nationale. Paris, 1848.

Chandon de Briailles, Raoul, and Henri Bertal, eds. Archives municipales d'Epernay, XVIe siècle. Paris, 1906.

Charron, Pierre. De la sagesse. Lyon, 1606.

Chasse au vieil grognard de l'antiquité (n.p., 1622), reprinted by Edouard Fournier in Variétés historiques et litteraires (Paris, 1853–63), III, 27–66.

Chérin, Louis-Nicolas-Henri. Abrégé chronologique d'édits, déclarations, règlements, arrêts et lettres patentes … concernant le fait de noblesse, as reprinted in J.-P. Migne, Nouvelle encyclopédie théologique, Vol. XIII. Paris, 1861.

———. La noblesse considérée sous ses divers rapports. Paris, 1788.

Coquille, Guy. Oeuvres. 2 vols. Paris, 1666.

Crest, Nicolas de (pseud.). Le cabinet du roy de France, dans lequel il y a trois perles precieuses. N.p., 1581.

Dallington, Sir Robert. The View of Fraunce, 1604. Oxford, 1936. Facsimile reprint of 1604 ed.

Descomel, Paul. Plaidoyé faict en la cour des aydes. Paris, 1625.

Des Osres, Jherome [Osorio, Jeronymo]. Les deux livres de la noblesse civile. Paris, 1549.

Discours d'un gentilhomme françois à la noblesse de France, sur l'ouverture de l'assemblée des états généraux dans la ville de Paris en ceste année 1614. N.p., [c. 1614].

Discours sur l'iniustice des plainctes qu'on faict contre le gouvernement de l'estat. N.p., [1625]. (Despite the indication of MDCXV on the title page, 1625 is a more likely date, since events of 1617 are mentioned on p. 23.)

Douais, Célestin, ed. Mémoires sur l'état du clergé, de la noblesse, de la justice et du peuple dans les diocèses de Narbonne, de Montpellier et de Castres en 1573. Toulouse, 1891.

Dubreuil, Joseph. Analyse raisonnée de la legislation sur les eaux. 2 vols. Aix, 1842.

Du devoir de la noblesse française vers son roy. N.p., 1594.

Du Fail, Noël. Contes et discours d'Eutrapel. Ed. C. Hippeau. 2 vols. Paris, 1875.

———. Oeuvres facétieuses. 2 vols. Paris, 1874.

Du Haillan, Bernard de Girard, Seigneur. De l'estat et succez des affaires de France. Rev. ed. Paris, 1609. First ed. 1570.

Du Rivault de Flurance, David. Les états, esquels il est discouru du prince, du noble, et du tiers estat. Lyon, 1596.

Du Vair, Guillaume. Oeuvres politiques, morales et meslées. Coligny, 1617.

Ernaud, Louis. Discours de la noblesse et des justes moyens d'y parvenir. Caen, 1584.

Les escritures et deffences des gents de la noblesse de Dauphiné. [Lyon, c. 1595.] Bound with La iuste plaincte . . . and La responce du tiers estat . . .

Fauchet, Claude. Oeuvres. Paris, 1610.

Fleuret, Fernand, and Louis Perceau, eds. Les satires françaises du XVIe siècle. Paris, 1922.

Fontanon, Antoine. Les édicts et ordonnances des rois de France. 3 vols. Paris, 1611.

Fourquevaux, Raymond, Baron de. "Discours au roy du compartement de ses sujets, 1574," in Dom Vaissette, Histoire générale de Languedoc, XII, 1065–88. Toulouse, 1890.

————. Instructions sur le faict de la guerre. Ed. G. Dickinson. London, 1954.

Frerot, Nicolas. Les basiliques ou edicts et ordonnances de roys de France. N.p., 1611.

Froumenteau, Nicolas (pseud.). Le secret des finances de France. 2d ed. N.p., 1581.

————. Le secret des thrésors de France. N.p., 1581.

Froydeville, Eymar de. Dialogues de l'origine de la noblesse. Lyon, 1574.

Grandmaison, Charles de, ed. Plaintes et doléances de la province de Touraine aux états-généraux. Tours, 1890.

Guénois, Pierre. La grande conférence des ordonnances. N.p., 1678.

Haton, Claude. Mémoires. Ed. Félix Bourquelot. 2 vols. Paris, 1857.

Imbert, Hugues. "Les Grands Jours de Poitiers: Registres criminels, 1531–1634," Mém. soc. de statistique, sciences, lettres et arts du Département des Deux-Sèvres. 2ᵉ sér., Vol. XVI (1878).

Inventaire sommaire des Archives Départementales antérieures à 1790. Haute-Garonne, Sér. C, t. II. Toulouse, 1903.

Isambert, François-André, *et al*. Recueil général des anciennes lois françaises. 29 vols. Paris, 1833.

La iuste plaincte et remonstrance faicte au roy . . . par le pauvre peuple de Daulphiné. Lyon, 1597.

Laffemas, Barthélemy de. Le plaisir de la noblesse et autres qui ont des éritages aux champs. Paris, 1603.

La Lande de Calan, Charles de, ed. Documents inédits relatifs aux états de Bretagne, 1491–1589. 2 vols. Rennes, 1908–9.

L'Alouëte, François de. Des affaires d'estat, des finances, du prince et de sa noblesse. Rev. ed. Metz, 1597.

————. Traité des nobles et des vertus dont ils sont formez. Paris, 1577. Reprinted, with few changes, as one section of *Affaires* in 1597.

La Loupe, Vincent de. Premier et second livre des dignitez, magistrats et offices du royaume de France. Paris, 1564. First published, in Latin, in 1551.

Lalourcé and Duval, eds. Recueil des cahiers généraux des trois ordres aux états généraux. 4 vols. Paris, 1789.

————. Recueil des pièces originales et authentiques concernant la tenue des états généraux. 9 vols. Paris, 1789.

La Noue, François de. Discours politiques et militaires. N.p., 1612. First ed., 1587.

La Perrière, Guillaume de. Le miroir politique, contenant diverses manières de gouverner et policer les republiques. Paris, 1567.

La Place, Pierre de. Traité de la vocation et manière de vivre à laquelle chacun est appelé. Paris, 1561.

La Planche, Regnier de. Histoire de l'estat de France. 2 vols. Paris, 1836. First ed., 1576.

La Roque, Gilles-André. Traité de la noblesse. N.p., 1678.

Le Bret, Cardin. Oeuvres. Rev. ed. Paris, 1688.

Le Caron, Louis. Pandectes ou digestes du droict françois. Rev. ed. Paris, 1637.

———. Responses et decisions du droict françois. Paris, 1637.

Le Masle, Jean. Le breviaire des nobles. Paris, 1578.

Leschassier, Jacques. Oeuvres. Paris, 1652.

Lettre missive d'un gentilhomme à un sien compagnon, contenant les causes du mescontentement de la noblesse de France. N.p., 1567.

Lettre servant d'apologie ou defense pour le premier plaidoyé du tiers estat de Dauphiné. [Paris, 1598.]

L'Hospital, Michel de. Oeuvres. Ed. P.-J.-S. Dufey. 5 vols. Paris, 1824–25.

Loyseau, Charles. Oeuvres. Lyon, 1701.

Marois, Claude de. Le gentilhomme parfait. Paris, 1631.

Mayer, Charles-Joseph de. Des états généraux et autres assemblées nationales. 19 vols. Paris, 1789.

Mayerne, Louis Turquet de. Apologie contre les détracteurs de livres de la monarchie aristodémocratique. N.p., 1617.

———. La monarchie aristodémocratique. Paris, 1611.

Mémoires de Condé. Ed. Secousse. 5 vols. London, 1743.

Monluc, Blaise de. Commentaires. Ed. Paul Courteault. 3 vols. Paris, 1911–25.

Montaigne, Michel de. Essays. Tr. E. J. Trechmann. Oxford, [1946].

Montand, Nicolas de (pseud.). Le miroir des françois. N.p., 1581.

Montchrétien, Antoyne de. Traicté de l'oeconomie politique. Ed. Théodore Funck-Brentano. Paris, 1889.

Musset, Louis. Discours sur les remontrances & reformation de chacun état. Paris, 1582.

Nenna, Jean-Baptiste [Nenna da Bari, Giovambattista]. Traicté de la noblesse. Paris, 1583.

Nostredamus, César de. "Discours de la noblesse," in L'Histoire et chronique de Provence. Lyon, 1624.

Oncieu, Guillaume d'. La précédence de la noblesse sus un différent en cas de précédence. Lyon, 1593.

Origny, Pierre d'. Le hérault de la noblesse de France. Reims, 1578.

Pasquier, Estienne. Oeuvres. 2 vols. Amsterdam, 1723.

Pasquier, Nicolas. Le gentilhomme. Paris, 1611.

Le paysan françois. N.p., n.d. Probably just before the Estates General of 1614.

Peleus, Julien. Oeuvres. Paris, 1638.

Piémond, Eustache. Mémoires d'Eustache Piémond. Ed. J. Brun-Durand. Valence, 1885.

Le plaidé des docteurs et advocats consistoriaux du parlement de Dauphiné, defendeurs, contre les demandes & pretentions du tiers estat dudit pais. Grenoble, 1599.

Plaidoyez pour le tiers estat du Dauphiné . . . contre les deux premiers ordres dudit pays. Paris, 1600.

Poncet, Maurice. Remontrance à la noblesse de France. Paris, 1572.

Pontaymery, Alexandre de. L'Academie ou institution de la noblesse françois. Paris, 1595.

Premieres escritures, pour la defence des nobles du Dauphiné contre les demandes & iniures du tiers estat dudit pais. N.p., n.d.

Ragueau, François. Indice des droits roiaux et seigneuriaux. Rev. ed. Paris, 1600.

Recueil des lettres missives de Henri IV. 9 vols. Paris, 1843–76.

Remonstrance aux François pour les induire à vivre en paix à l'advenir. N.p., 1576.

Remonstrance faicte par deux cents gentilshommes français au chancelier. N.p., 1615.

Responce à une lettre envoyée par un gentilhomme de basse Bretagne à un sien amy estant à la suitte de la cour sur le misere de ce temps. Rouen, n.d.

La responce du tiers estat et commun peuple aux escriptures du second estat & gents de la noblesse de Daulphiné. Lyon, 1595.

Response à une lettre escrite à Compiegne du quatrième jour d'aoust, touchant le mescontentement de la noblesse de France. N.p., 1567.

Richebourg, Charles A. Bourdot de, ed. Nouveau coutumier général. 4 vols. Paris, 1724.

Richelieu, Armand-Jean de Plessis, Cardinal de. Testament politique. Ed. Louis André. Paris, 1947.

Robillard de Beaurepaire, Charles de, ed. Cahiers des états de Normandie. Rouen, 1871–88.

Second plaidoyé pour le tiers estat du Dauphiné. Paris, 1600.
Secondes escritures pour l'estat des nobles du Dauphiné. N.p., n.d.
Seyssel, Claude de. La grand monarchie de France. Paris, 1557. First ed., 1515.

Thierriat, Florentin de. Trois traités; de la noblesse de race, de la noblesse civile & des immunitez des ignobles. Paris, 1606.
Tholin, Georges, ed. Cahier des doléances du tiers état du pays d'Agenais aux états généraux. Paris, 1885.
Tiraqueau, André. Tractatus de nobilitate. Paris, 1549.
Tommaseo, N., ed. Relations des ambassadeurs vénitiens sur les affaires de France. 2 vols. Paris, 1838.

Vaissette, Dom, et al. Histoire générale de Languedoc. 16 vols. Toulouse, 1873–1905.
Valles, Claude de. Au roy et à nosseigneurs de son conseil. N.p., n.d.
———. Mémoires et instructions pour établir en ce royaume un règlement sur les abus qui se commettent sur le fait des armoiries. Paris, 1629.
———. Mémoire succinct, dressé sur un règlement des armoiries en ce royaume. N.p., n.d.
La vérité des justes defences de la noblesse du Dauphiné. N.p., n.d.
Vieilleville, François de (pseud.). Mémoires. 5 vols. Paris, 1757.

BIBLIOGRAPHICAL NOTES TO CHAPTERS

INTRODUCTION. Among the several older works on the nobility of the sixteenth and seventeenth centuries that contain some valuable evidence and references are Henri Baudrillart, *Gentilshommes ruraux de la France* (Paris, 1894); Vicomte Georges d'Avenel, *La noblesse française sous Richelieu* (Paris, 1901); and Pierre Vaissière, *Gentilshommes campagnards de l'ancienne France*, 2d ed. (Paris, 1925). Works that consider the nobility's problems as one aspect of a general crisis include Claude de Bonnault, "La société française au XVIe siècle, 1515–1614," *Bulletin de recherches historiques*, LXII (1956), 21–28, 76–87; Fernand Braudel, *La Mediterranée et le monde mediterranéen à l'époque de Philippe II* (Paris, 1949); Philippe Sagnac, *La formation de la société française moderne*, 2 vols. (Paris, n.d.); and Robert Mandrou, *Introduction à la France moderne, 1500–1640: Essai de psychologie historique* (Paris, 1961).

For the relationship between the nobility and the monarchy, see Giuliano Procacci, *Classi sociali e monarchia assoluta nella Francia della prima metà del secolo XVI* (Turin, 1955); Pierre Deyon, "A propos des rapports entre la noblesse française et la monarchie absolue pendant la première moitié du XVIIe siècle," *Revue historique*, CCXXXI (1964), 341-56; J. Russell Major, "The Crown and the Aristocracy in Renaissance France," *American Historical Review*, LXIX (1964), 631-45; and Orest Ranum, "Richelieu and the Great Nobility," *French Historical Studies*, III (1963), 184-204. Roland Mousnier, "L'Evolution des institutions monarchiques en France et ses relations avec l'état social," *XVIIe Siècle*, Nos. 58-59 (1963), pp. 57-72, sees conflict among the three orders as one of the conditions facilitating a strong monarchy. Standard treatments of French institutions of the sixteenth century, with good chapters on military, judicial, and administrative practices, are Roger Doucet, *Les institutions de la France au XVIe siècle* (Paris, 1948); and Gaston Zeller, *Les institutions de la France au XVIe siècle* (Paris, 1948).

CHAPTER I. The point of departure for the study of peasant revolts (although Georges Pagès and others earlier touched on the question) is Boris Porchnev, *Les soulèvements populaires en France de 1623 à 1648* (Paris, 1963; original Russian edition, 1948), which portrays the revolts as protests by an oppressed peasantry against both aristocracy and monarchy. The main opposition to this interpretation has come from Roland Mousnier, in a series of articles written over the last decade, beginning with "Recherches sur les soulèvements populaires en France avant la Fronde," *Revue d'histoire moderne et contemporaine*, Vol. V (1958); his most recent work is *Fureurs paysannes: Les paysans dans les révoltes du XVIIe siècle* (1968). Mousnier demonstrated that in many instances the peasants were encouraged and even supported by the nobility. See especially on this point his "Monarchie contre aristocratie dans la France du XVIIe siècle," *XVIIe Siècle*, No. 31 (1956), pp. 377-81. However, the article also shows that relations were not always the best between the peasants and their seigneurs. I do not believe that Mousnier wishes to argue that the revolts always found the nobles and peasants working together—which would be to replace one extreme interpretation by another. J. H. M. Salmon notes that "the desire to refute Porchnev's interpretation, and to find the local nobility and officials, rather than the peasants, responsible for the uprising, may have resulted in some over-simplification." See "Venality of Office and Popular Sedition in 17th Century France," *Past and Present*, No. 37 (1967), pp. 21–43. There are many indications of the peasants' animosity toward the nobles during the sixteenth and seventeenth centuries, and this animosity was sometimes an element in peasant revolts.

Elizabeth Salmon Teall, "The Seigneur of Renaissance France: Advocate or Oppressor?" *Journal of Modern History*, XXXVII (1965), 131–50, rightly recognizes that the seigneurs were very often solicitous of their peasants. But this can be conceded while maintaining that there was resentment, which was intensified when the nobles—old or new—tried to increase revenue by more forceful exploitation of seigneurial dues. Mrs. Teall does not maintain that all nobles were magnanimous and paternalistic, and it is hard to believe that such behavior was typical, in light of the outbursts described above in Chapter 1.

Among recent works that add details and refinements are Claude Galarneau, "La mentalité paysanne en France sous l'Ancien Régime," *Revue d'histoire de l'Amérique française*, XIV (1960), 16–24; Louis Jasseron, "Les Grands Jours de Lyon en 1596," *Tout Lyon*, No. 724 (1963), pp. 1–2; No. 726 (1963), pp. 1–3; Françoise Bercé, "Exactions des gens de guerre, 1625-1626," *Bulletin historique, scientifique, littéraire artistique et agricole illustré publié par la société académique du Puys*, XXXIX (1962), 50–55; Y.-M. Bercé, "De la criminalité aux troubles sociaux: La noblesse rurale du Sud-Ouest de la France sous Louis XIII," *Annales du Midi*, LXXVI (1964), 42–59; Vital Chomel, "Seigneurs et paysans de Chapeau-Cornu au début du XVIIe siècle," *Evocations*, new series, VII (1965), 83–95; and E. Nolin, "Episodes de la 'lutte des classes' à Dijon au XVIe siècle," *Annales de Bourgogne*, XXXVI (1964), 270–75. Nolin shows how complex the alignments often were. He found that in the 1520's there was endemic hostility between two groups: *vignerons* and craftsmen on one side, nobles, churchmen, bourgeois, jurists, and some merchants on the other. Even this early, as Nolin demonstrates, violence could be triggered by pretensions of noble superiority.

Since the controversy in Dauphiny provided considerable evidence of class hostilities, it may be helpful to see a review article by Vital Chomel, "Le Dauphiné sous l'Ancien Régime," *Cahiers d'histoire publiés par les Universités de Clermont, Lyon, Grenoble,* VIII (1963), 303–39. I have not yet seen the following doctoral thesis written at the University of Paris, but it almost certainly contains relevant information: Pierre-Henri Chaix, "La noblesse protestante du Dauphiné du 16ᵉ au 18ᵉ siècle."

The legal complexities of taille réelle and the inconsistent ways the term has been used are elucidated by Edmond Esmonin in *Etudes sur la France des XVIIᵉ et XVIIIᵉ siècles* (Paris, 1964).

CHAPTER 2. A close analysis of recruitment, mercenary contracts, changes in the officer cadre, and social class divisions is still, to my knowledge, unavailable. For the large trends, especially during the early seventeenth century, see Michael Roberts, *The Military Revolution, 1560–1660* (1956), which treats France only in the European context. Jean Pablo, "Contribution à l'étude de l'histoire des institutions militaires huguenotes. II. L'armée huguenote entre 1562 et 1573," *Archiv für Reformationsgeschichte,* XLVIII (1957), 192–216, provides some important refinements. The Huguenot infantry included not only social outcasts but artisans and even bourgeois, whereas the cavalry included some urban elements besides the traditional nobles. In noting the large number of mercenaries employed by both Huguenot and Catholic forces, Pablo accepts the view that the raising of native troops was discouraged by the nobility's fears of uprisings. See also A. Gouron, "Le ban et l'arrière-ban d'après les sources languedociennes," *27ᵉ–28ᵉ Congrès fédération historique de Languedoc* (1956), pp. 87–100.

CHAPTER 3. Examination of the old nobility's efforts to retain or regain offices must start with Roland Mousnier, *La vénalité des offices sous Henri IV et Louis XIII* (Rouen, [1946]). Orest Ranum, *Richelieu and the councillors of Louis XIII* (Oxford, 1963), contains relevant information on this topic. On the Estates General of 1614, see George A. Rothrock, "Officials and King's Men: A Note on the Possibility of Royal Control in the Estates General," *French Historical Studies,* II (1962), 504–10; J. Michael Hayden, "Deputies and *Qualités*: The Estates General of 1614," *French Historical Studies,* III (1964), 507–24; and J. Russell Major, *The Deputies to the Estates General in Renaissance France* (Madison, Wisconsin, 1960). Salvo Mastellone, *La Reggenza di Maria de' Medici* (Florence, 1962) contains a valuable chapter on "I pubblici ufficiali rappresentanti del terzo stato." See also the titles under Chapter 6, below.

CHAPTER 4. The question of attitudes toward industry and commerce continues to excite interest, perhaps because of its relevance to the idea of an "entrepreneurial spirit," which certain economists have seen as essential to the achievement of economic growth. Recent treatments of the French nobility's relationship to commerce and the influence of the rule of dérogeance are R. B. Grassby, "Social Status and Commercial Enterprise under Louis XIV," *Economic History Review*, series 2, XIII (1960), 19–38; Betty Behrens, "Nobles, Privileges and Taxes in France at the End of the Ancien Régime," *Economic History Review*, series 2, XV (1963), 451–75; Jacqueline Hecht, "Un problème de population active au XVIIIe siècle en France: La querelle de la noblesse commerçante," *Population*, XIX (1964), 267–90; Etienne Dravasa, " 'Vivre noblement': Recherches sur la dérogeance de la noblesse du XIVe au XVIe siècle," *Revue juridique et économique du Sud-ouest, série juridique*, XVI (1965), 135–93; and Guy Richard, "Un aspect particulier de la politique économique et sociale de la monarchie au XVIIe siècle," *XVIIe Siècle*, No. 49 (1960), pp. 11–41. A good summary of the "intelligible and in some respects valid reasons for the refusal of the noblesse d'épée" to enter commerce is in A. Goodwin, "The Social Origins and Privileged Status of the French Eighteenth-Century Nobility," *Bulletin of the John Rylands Library*, XLVII (1965), 400–1.

CHAPTER 5. The concepts of "virtue and "birth" as they entered into discussion of the nobility during our period reflected changing moral values. For the large setting, see Eugene F. Rice, *The Renaissance Idea of Wisdom* (Cambridge, Mass., 1958), and Aldo Vallone, *Cortesia e nobiltà nel Rinascimento* (Asti, 1955). The extent to which issues discussed in Renaissance treatises on nobility were at once conventional and related to actual social conditions is well explained by Charity Cannon Willard, "The Concept of True Nobility at the Burgundian Court," *Studies in the Renaissance*, XIV (1967), 33–48.

CHAPTER 6. Questions about the meaning of noble status require consideration of social mobility, numbers and kinds of new nobles, and terminology. See Franklin L. Ford, *Robe and Sword: The Regrouping of the French Aristocracy after Louis XIV* (Cambridge,

Mass., 1953), even though it focuses on the early eighteenth century. Important for its methodological discussion is Robert Mandrou, "Un exemple de définition: Le concept de classe," *2ᵉ Conférence Internationale d'histoire économique*, Aix-en-Provence, 1962, 2 vols. (Paris, 1965), II, 829–35. Insights into the tensions in the mid-seventeenth century are presented by Roland Mousnier, J. P. Labatut, and Y. Durand, *Problèmes de stratification sociale: Deux cahiers de la noblesse pour les Etats Généraux de 1649–1651* (Paris, 1965).

Prejudice against the assertive bourgeoisie and noble insistence on maintaining an obsolete self-image are treated by Jean V. Alter, *Les origines de la satire anti-bourgeoise en France* (Geneva, 1966).

Local or regional studies of the officeholding class include René Fédou, *Les hommes de lois lyonnais á la fin du moyen âge. Etude sur les origines de la classe de robe* (Paris, 1964); H. de Frondeville, *Les conseillers du parlement de Normandie sous Henri IV et Louis XIII, 1594–1640* (Rouen, 1964); and J. C. Paulhet, "Les parlementaires toulousains à la fin du XVIIᵉ siècle," *Annales du Midi*, LXXVI (1964), 189–204. The social status of the bourgeoisie, its offices, its purchase of estates, and intermarriage with the old aristocracy, are explored in many local studies, including Janine Estèbe, "La bourgeoisie marchande et la terre à Toulouse au XVIᵉ siècle (1519–1560)," *Annales du Midi*, LXXVI (1964), 457–67; Romain Baron, "La bourgeoisie de Varzy au XVIIᵉ siècle," *Annales de Bourgogne*, XXVI (1964), 161–208; and Janine Fayard, "L'Ascension sociale d'une famille de bourgeois parisiens au XVIIᵉ siècle: Les Bidal d'Asfeld," *Bulletin de la société de l'histoire de Paris et de l'Ile-de-France*, XC (1965), 84–110. The social, political, and economic fortunes of one office are examined in Jean-Paul Charmeil, *Les trésoriers de France á l'époque de la Fronde* (Paris, 1964).

BIBLIOGRAPHICAL ESSAY ON THE ECONOMIC
FORTUNES OF THE NOBILITY

Recent works have challenged the traditional views of "the decline of the aristocracy." Although they did not deal with the French nobility, J. H. Hexter's observations in 1955 about the continued domination of a landed aristocracy in England up to the eighteenth century and beyond (*Reappraisals in History* [1961], pp. 18–25) cast doubt on facile generalizations about other aristoc-racies. In 1960, Robert Forster published *The Nobility of Toulouse in the Eighteenth Century: A Social and Economic Study* (Balti-more, Md.), which includes some specific estimates of nobles' in-comes. In 1750, he calculated, the average landed estate produced a revenue of about three thousand livres. Supplemented from other sources — judicial offices, *rentes*, royal pensions — this income climbed during the latter half of the century. By 1789, he concluded, the average noble income was at least eight thousand livres, which was "two to three times the revenue of a prosperous merchant, a retired bourgeois, or a successful lawyer at Toulouse." The tradi-tional image of an impoverished nobility during the period of the Old Regime obviously required some modification, at least for Toulouse in the eighteenth century. Later, J. Russell Major, in "The French Renaissance Monarchy as seen through the Estates General," *Studies in the Renaissance,* IX (1962), 113–35, tried to extend the revisionist interpretation back to the sixteenth century. The monarchy, he argued, was inherently weak and dependent on the support of the subjects, especially the nobility. The nobility he described as "dynamic" in wresting concessions from the crown. And "many" nobles, he said, increased rather than decreased their revenues.

But when we turn to other local and regional studies, it becomes clear that scholars are still far from a consensus. Olwen H. Hufton, *Bayeux in the Late Eighteenth Century: A Social Study* (Oxford, 1967) finds that the urban noble families of Bayeux, about a hun-dred in number, included two or three very wealthy families and about fifty families with incomes roughly equivalent to those of the wealthy bourgeois. But three important facts deserve to be no-ticed. (1) Most of these urban nobles had entered the aristocracy rather recently, through judicial positions which they had now abandoned. It makes a difference, obviously, whether a class is de-fined in terms of old families that are being displaced or in terms of the new wealth that is buying up estates; this distinction, similar in some ways to the problem of definition that has plagued the scholarly "Storm over the Gentry" in English history, is not always carefully made by revisionist scholars. (2) Even among the urban nobility of Bayeux there was an appreciable minority, some 17 fami-lies, on the economic level of poor tradesmen and wool carders.

(3) As Hufton suggests (p. 56), the condition of the town noble was considerably better than that of the small parish seigneur out in the country. Other studies, such as Jean Beyer's *La noblesse bretonne au XVIIIᵉ siècle* (Paris, 1966), should make us skeptical of any supposed general prosperity of the nobility in the eighteenth century.

Other local and regional histories comment on the economic fortunes of the nobility in the late sixteenth and early seventeenth centuries. They suggest that the traditional interpretation lacks refinement, but they are far from rejecting the whole idea of a "declining" nobility. Gaston Roupnel, in *La ville et la campagne au XVIIᵉ siècle: Etude sur les populations du pays dijonnais* (Paris, 1955), p. 234, shows that the land market definitely included a large-scale transfer of lands from old noble families to rich bourgeois:

What caused the transfer of land to the urban bourgeoisie was the impoverishment of the nobility, which had been ruined by war, economic activity, and the fall in the value of money.

The old seigneurial family, which lived in the noble style and had no surplus capital, was driven out of existence by the rich bourgeoisie except where it was adroit enough to obtain offices at court or prudent enough to acquire them in town.

Although this trend started in the fifteenth century and extended over several generations, Roupnel recognizes the crucial importance of the period of this study: "Thus it was toward the end of the sixteenth century that the most advantageous and most numerous transfers of land were made, to the profit of the bourgeois. It was the period when the old nobility underwent the crisis that finally dispossessed it." (p. 235.)

In his view of the long-range ruin of the nobility, and of their loss of noble estates, as in his description of noble indebtedness, Roupnel accepts and reinforces the traditional interpretation of the nobility's time of troubles. He does recognize that the amount of revenue from land depended on methods of exploitation and tenure. He sees a basic difference between the "new" noble, a businessman determined to make his estates pay economically as well as socially, and the old noble, who usually preferred fixed payments to the troublesome administration and uncertainties of more flexible methods of exploitation: "They adjusted their lives to the regular receipt of these meager revenues; and they preferred accepting little to taking the chance of less." (p. 310.) This choice inevitably led to the ruin of those who made it: "Only those survived whose landholdings were sufficiently great to enable them to withstand these incursions." (p. 312.) Although conditions generally began to improve for some nobles in the eighteenth century, by then few of the old families remained: "Of the old seigneurial families, very few survived the crises of the sixteenth and seventeenth centuries." (p. 313.)

Another recent regional history, edited by Philippe Wolff, *Histoire du Languedoc* (Toulouse, 1967), upholds the traditional view of a pinched and weakened aristocracy. E. LeRoy Ladurie, one of the contributors, after describing the various kinds of seigneurial dues of the sixteenth century, remarks that the seigneury "is almost nonexistent as a source of wealth: it is only a dead arm of the economy." The traditional view of declining estate incomes in the sixteenth century may be a commonplace, but it nevertheless has some validity:

It is a commonplace to describe the gradual decline and fall of the landed nobility in the West, slowly choked to death in the sixteenth century by the revolution in prices, which devalued and ultimately eliminated the income yielded by their estates: in Languedoc, this commonplace describes a very real situation, especially in the vicinity of the towns.

The question remains whether the seigneurs were able to recoup their losses by exploiting their personal domains. This depended entirely, says LeRoy Ladurie, on the kind of lease. Lands leased on a share-of-crop basis, to métayers, brought in a rising income throughout the century, even a rising percentage of the yield as competition among métayers resulted from the population pressures. Lands leased for a fixed payment, either in produce or money, did not bring in the same increasing returns. Although the leases were for limited periods, usually three, six, or nine years, and thus were theoretically subject to renegotiation at frequent intervals, the rents did not actually move upward during the century. To the extent that his domain lands were thus farmed out, a seigneur would indeed have suffered from a relatively fixed income in a period of rising prices. We are not told what percentages of noble lands were in each of these different categories, but this "réponse mitigée" does delineate some of the complexities of the problem.

Robert Mandrou has suggested in *Histoire de la civilisation française* (Paris, 1958), p. 307, that noble complaints were due to rising expenditures even though their incomes were increasing:

> In fact, their nominal gains, though incontestable, seemed to them of little value for several reasons: because they had been "eaten up" by rises in the prices of products they bought—tapestries woven of silk and gold, fine woollens, paintings, furniture—... which had risen in price no less than grain; and above all because the nobility had become insatiable consumers of these products, the luxury goods of their time. ... They forgot their gains in the face of such great expenses, such endlessly increasing needs. ... Thus we find the landholders, noble and clerical alike, ungrateful beneficiaries of the economic revolution.

To say that the price of luxury goods went up "not less" than the price of grain does not tell us, of course, whether or not it went up more. We really need more than a general assertion that nobles' incomes were rising. Where? When? By how much? In real or merely monetary value? But the kinds and amounts of expenditures by nobles are obviously important variables to consider.

Another thorough local study is Pierre Goubert's *Beauvais et le Beauvaisis de 1600 à 1730: Contribution à l'histoire sociale de la France du XVIIe siècle* (Paris, 1960). Goubert has no doubt that the economic condition of the nobility in this region was generally deplorable: "A good third of the noble families of the bailliage were able to enter what is called the ranks of the shameful poor; it is, besides, certain that several among them subsisted only by means of discreet charity." (p. 213.) After considering the general trend of the land market, through which wealthy urban families habitually acquired land at the expense of indebted nobles, Goubert concludes: "No fact of the social order is more striking and more widespread than the indebtedness of the nobility, than the transfer of nobles' goods into the hands of bourgeois creditors, Beauvaisiens or Parisiens, than the slow but steady infiltration of the rich bourgeoisie into the lands, the châteaux, the families, and the ranks of the nobles of the area." Goubert does not consider the price revolution alone to be an adequate explanation of the nobility's economic plight. More important was the way the nobles administered their estates. The decline in income had started at least as early as the sixteenth century, and then the religious wars left many noble families destitute; when to this was added the style of living of a status-conscious nobility, the result, Goubert thinks, was inescapable. He is not at all inclined to reject the picture of the nobility as an economically impoverished class.

It is apparent that historians disagree about the consequences of the economic trends for the noble class. Part of the difficulty is semantic. For example, if a merchant bought up the estates of an impoverished noble family, continuing to exact—perhaps even more vigorously—the seigneurial dues, if he had letters of ennoblement or was affiliated with offices of robe longue, if his children or grandchildren intermarried with established aristocratic families, there may have been little enough change from the point of view of the peasants. A few families' losing their status or a weakening of one faction of the noble class was not tantamount to a decline of the aristocracy in the large sense. A landed seigneurial class did indeed continue to dominate society in many respects through the seventeenth and eighteenth centuries. But what we have been concerned with in the present work, following the testimony of contemporary writers, is primarily the *old* nobility. Thus when the word "noblesse" is used alone, we are usually safe in inferring the qualifying epithets "ancienne" or "d'épée." When the claims of revisionists regarding the nobility's supposed continuing prosperity and vigor are examined carefully, on the other hand, it is apparent that they have usually included the parvenus, the "new" nobility.

It is difficult to make statements about the Old Regime without suggesting uniformity by that label. But it is clear that there were important regional differences within France. For our present purposes we can concede that the French nobility of the sixteenth and seventeenth centuries was not universally and inevitably suffering because of rising prices. Some families maintained themselves through thick and thin. But there is enough evidence for the opposite situation to show that the nobility as a class was not fundamentally prosperous. For the provincial noblesse d'épée, the families of the old nobility, the period was one of economic difficulty and, for many, genuine hardship. Until further research is done on chronological trends, regional variations, and differences among subgroups of the aristocracy, perhaps this guarded generalization, for which reputable historians continue to find evidence, best enables us to understand the pamphlets, cahiers, and treatises discussed here.

Index